THE JOURNEY TO FINDING INNER SAFETY

Exercises to Increase Nervous System Strength & Resilience

LENORA KLASSEN, DPT

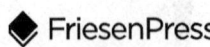
 FriesenPress

One Printers Way
Altona, MB R0G 0B0
Canada

www.friesenpress.com

Copyright © 2024 by Lenora Klassen, DPT
First Edition — 2024

All rights reserved.

No part of this publication may be reproduced in any form, or by any means, electronic or mechanical, including photocopying, recording, or any information browsing, storage, or retrieval system, without permission in writing from FriesenPress.

Image: © Loraine Ehresman - Surrey Portrait Photographer

ISBN
978-1-03-830095-9 (Hardcover)
978-1-03-830094-2 (Paperback)
978-1-03-830096-6 (eBook)

1. SELF-HELP, SELF-MANAGEMENT, STRESS MANAGEMENT

Distributed to the trade by The Ingram Book Company

In honour of those who have journeyed through the pain of trauma. May we rise to find the strength we had all along.

Special thanks to my cheerleaders. You know who you are!

TABLE OF CONTENTS

Introduction 1
    How to Use This Book 4

Getting to Know Your Nervous System 7
    Polyvagal Theory and the Vagus Nerve 9
    Safety First 11
    How a Resilient Nervous System Can Help You 12
    Know Your Window of Tolerance 16
        Awareness Exercises for Nervous System
        Safety and Resilience 18
    Building Guardrails for Your Nervous System 19
        Vagus Nerve Stimulation Exercises 20
        Finding Your Safe Anchors 20
        Using Your Anchors 21
        Know Your States 22
    Body Awareness 22
    Interoception 23

Building Safety and Resilience Through the Body 25
    Mindfulness 26
        Mindfulness Exercises for Nervous System
        Safety and Resilience 28
    Breathing 30
        Breathing Exercises for Nervous System
        Safety and Resilience 32
    Body Movement 34
        Movement Exercises for Nervous System
        Safety and Resilience 35
    Stretching 39
        Stretching Exercises for Nervous System
        Safety and Resilience 40

Strengthening 42
   Strengthening Exercises for Nervous System
   Safety and Resilience 44
Balance and Proprioception........................... 46
   Balance and Proprioception Exercises for
   Nervous System Safety and Resilience 47
Posture 50
   Posture Exercises for Nervous System
   Safety and Resilience 51

Building Safety and Resilience Through Nutrition 55
   Inflammatory Foods 56
   Sugars 57
   Chemical Foods 59
   Supplements and Medications 59
   Caffeine and Stimulants 60
   Generalities 60
The Food We Eat 61
   Stress Eating 62
   Elimination Tips 63
   Nutrition Exercises for Nervous System
   Safety and Resilience 65
Hydration 67
   How to Hydrate 68
   Sodium 69
   Elimination 70
   Hydration Exercises for Nervous System
   Safety and Resilience 71

Building Safety and Resilience with Your Life 73
Sleep 74
   Preparing Your Nervous System for Sleep 76
   Preparing Your Nervous System for Wakefulness 77

    Practical Tips to Encourage
    Neurological Safety in Sleep 78
    Sleeping Positions. 79
    Sleep Exercises for Nervous System
    Safety and Resilience 81
Social Connection 84
    Connection Exercises for Nervous System
    Safety and Resilience 86
Boundaries. 88
    Boundary Exercises for Nervous System
    Safety and Resilience 88
Play 91
    How Does Play Strengthen Our Nervous System? 92
    Forms of Play 93
    Is Gaming a Therapeutic Form of Play?. 95
    Playfulness Exercises for Nervous System
    Safety and Resilience 96
Spirituality. 99
    Spirituality Exercises for Nervous System
    Safety and Resilience 101

Conclusion. 105

Additional Resources 107

Glossary of Terms 109

Introduction

IT IS THE JOURNEY OF a lifetime. Like all good journeys, it has a destination, some preparation, supplies, and a map on how to get there. The destination of this journey is one of inner safety. From this vantage point, we can see other paths to healing. We can see and experience the beauty in this world. We can appreciate the strength it took to get there. But I propose that inner safety is both the destination and the first step.

How can nervous system safety be described? Like the flight of a kite anchored to the earth yet soaring in the wind? The saying "stay calm and carry on"? Somehow illustrations fall flat. Safety is felt and experienced, it is not taught. So, how will I write a book teaching inner safety? I will do that by going on the journey with you.

Finding safety within might seem like a lofty goal, or maybe entirely confusing. Perhaps you have never considered whether you feel safe within your own self. Or maybe you have an acute awareness of how dangerous or uncertain you feel inside. Either way, this book was written for you.

We each have a unique relationship with our own self. This may have been influenced by our family of origin, or our childhood. Or our unsafe relationship with ourselves might be largely influenced by a history of physical injury or emotional trauma. We might feel safety in our emotional self, but not our physical self, or vice versa or neither.

Whatever has brought you to this point, you are reading this book because there was something interesting about the idea of finding more safety within yourself.

What does safety look like? A sense of safety in self will have a sense of peace, of compassion, and understanding. Safety allows us to be fully present, not stuck in the past, or fretting over the future. When we are in safety, we can savour the experiences we are having right now.

Safety is also the starting point for developing resilience. Resilience is the ability to meet a changing world and adapt to it. This is often thought of as the ability to overcome obstacles, but resilience is also the ability to accept opportunities. Stepping into a new thing in life is as much a celebration of resilience as overcoming a hardship. In this book, we will explore practical ways to build that capacity.

In our journey together, we will learn a little more about our nervous system and develop a safer and more compassionate relationship with ourselves. This is an experiential journey; learning what safety feels like in many aspects of life. We learn by doing.

We will journey through a trauma-informed path to reconnect with our nervous system, learning its language, and challenging it in small, deliberate ways to increase our resilience in life. The steps we take will be incremental, but there will be ways for anyone to challenge their nervous system to gain greater safety and resilience.

If we have been under stress for a long time, we may not remember what it feels like to be resilient. Resilience allows us to withstand a greater amount of stimulus before "failure." In this context, resilience means that when stress comes, we are more easily able to return to a place of safety and calm. It also means that we can tolerate a greater stress before our system is activated or panicked. For example, for someone with anxiety, a book dropping to the floor can cause a startle reflex. It is not a thought out process. It reflects a high level of activation in our nervous system. Increasing resilience means that we may not startle with those sudden sounds. Or, if we do, the startle won't be as dramatic, and will be easier to calm after the startle.

Our nervous system is designed to respond to threats in our outside world. It responds with one ultimate goal: survival! Some of us have had times in our lives where it seems that our survival was hanging on by a thread. We had to claw our way out of dire situations. And then we look back at those seasons and wonder how we did it. Where did the strength come from? How did we manage to do that? The greatest lesson I learned from my years in university was not the lessons in the textbooks but the resilience I experienced after an exam week that I didn't know how I'd make it through, and yet, I did, repeatedly.

Somehow, through those moments of survival, you develop greater strength and resilience. Perhaps looking back at a stressful time, it might not seem as catastrophic as it did in the moment. This is likely not because you were overreacting when you were going through your difficult time. It is likely because you came out stronger. This book speaks to that process of gaining inner strength; rather than waiting for those big stressful times to teach you resilience, you can do it now, in smaller, deliberate ways.

Perhaps you are currently in one of those moments of hanging on by a thread. I get it. I've been there. My hope is that there might be something helpful in this book. It was written for those who are totally overwhelmed, as well as for those who are doing well but want more from life.

It is my heartfelt wish that this is a beautiful journey of transforming your nervous system. It is also my wish that your more resilient nervous system will be the stepping stone to greater health and a greater life.

How to Use This Book

This book is not a complete guide to healing trauma, or a complete guide to your nervous system. There are plenty of great authors who have contributed immensely to the field of nervous system regulation. You will meet several of them as I reference their contributions in this book either directly or in the additional resources list if you want to delve deeper into a specific area.

This book is designed to be an easy-access book to quickly get you to some practical exercises to help reacquaint yourself with inner safety and to start the process of building resilience. I do that by offering some basic information on a wide range of topics that relate to how your nervous system functions. Then I will give some practical tips in these areas as low-hanging fruit; easily incorporated suggestions that will make the exercises easier to start and become more effective. Finally, I will give exercises specifically connecting your nervous system to that aspect of your life.

I wrote this book as a response to the needs I've seen in my physiotherapy practice. As my skills grew, I saw more and more complicated clients with difficult-to-treat chronic pain. Seeking ways to help them, I gained a greater understanding of the role of our nervous system in our healing process. While this is more obvious in the psychological world of healing trauma, an understanding of nervous system states is not widely included as basic training in the world of physical healing, such as physiotherapy.

This means that traditional physiotherapy and other healing modalities run the risk of adding trauma or causing nervous system dysregulation through pure ignorance or a desperation to meet aggressive goals from clients, therapists, and insurance companies. Ironically, this often prolongs the healing process, further frustrating everyone involved.

The study of the treatment of chronic pain has led to some improvements in the way we treat patients. We now know that the body affects mental and emotional health and vice versa. We feel emotions physically and we react mentally and emotionally to physical things such as pain or disability. It is with this in mind that I propose starting first with the physical body, the outside container of life; then the internal substance of nutrition; and finally with aspects of life itself. This is the structure of this journey. My hope is that this book will provide a very basic look at many aspects of life and health, to allow you to see the common thread of nervous system health in each aspect, reflecting into other aspects. You will find sections on physical health, nutritional health, and other habits of life including sleep and play.

This journey will give you practical tools to help build a more resilient and adaptable nervous system that will allow you to make the desired healing changes. It does not replace therapies such as physiotherapy, massage therapy, chiropractic, counselling, or naturopathic care for example. If you have health care needs, you should maintain those practitioners on your team.

Your nervous system guides your life in powerful ways. It wants to protect you and preserve your life. But there are situations that teach the nervous system that you are still under attack even when you are not. We need an adaptable nervous system. It needs to identify threats when they come, but also to identify when they are no longer a threat, and when you can move back into a state of safety.

The goal with the exercises provided, is to build a nervous system that can more easily come back to safety after it's been activated. The first chapter highlights some guardrails and awareness exercises to keep you in your best window to make changes in your nervous system and to ensure that you are not pushing yourself too fast, causing more harm than good. The first step exercises are designed to establish safety. Think, "safety first." It would be helpful to practise the first step exercises in a variety of categories before moving on to any of the "next steps" or "advanced steps." The goal is to challenge the system but not trigger yourself.

Once you feel confident with many of the first step exercises, you may want to spend extra time doing more exercises with a topic that you struggle with. Keep in mind that these topics will likely require more time, more practical tips, and even some additional resourcing like manual therapy, naturopathy, or medical advice, etc. If you seem to stall in your progression, it might be helpful to do some of the exercises in another topic. The goal is not to master a topic but to build your nervous system as a whole. That can be done in any of the topics if you are doing the exercises that feel challenging but not triggering. Because we are affecting the nervous system, improvement in one area will help other areas.

My hope is that you will feel some greater ease in your life as you connect and listen to your nervous system and as you are able to savour the sensation of safety from within. Welcome to your journey to finding greater safety in self.

Getting to Know Your Nervous System

OUR NERVOUS SYSTEM RUNS THROUGH our entire body. It tells our brain everything it needs to know about the systems of our body and the space we are in. It gives instructions about what is safe or not safe, which muscles to contract for a certain movement, and gives instructions to tell our heart to beat. Our nervous system runs our lives.

The many aspects of our nervous system can be divided into two categories. The *somatic nervous system* includes the parts that are under the control of our decision-making brain. This system decides which muscles to contract to raise our arm, or how to solve a puzzle. The *autonomic nervous system* is the part that happens automatically. It detects and prepares for danger, it digests food into usable energy, and it makes our heart beat faster when we see someone we love. These functions are automatic and reflexive. This means that the responses happen so fast that our cognitive brain does not have time to override them, like telling us not to jump at a startling moment of a scary movie.

Our autonomic nervous system has one goal in mind, to keep us alive. When we are at peace, with no danger to our lives, our autonomic nervous system is calmly busy with the moment-by-moment tasks of digestion, breathing, pumping blood, and regulating the levels of the various hormones and other substances that are needed for optimal life. In this state, our autonomic nervous system builds the resources it needs for times of increased stress.

When we face stress, threat, or danger, our nervous system diverts energy from the regular health functions to bring more energy to our arms and legs so we can fight or flee. This is a state of action, present action, or anticipating action. The system that does this is called the sympathetic nervous system. Physically, we may feel this as anxiety or nervousness. In this state, it might be difficult to be still and calm, because our nervous system is prepared to run away from danger.

The *sympathetic nervous system* state is one of activation. Activation with and without danger are similar but not the same. In the face of danger, a part of the brain called the amygdala fires to let the brain know about it. At that moment, primitive, quick, and reflexive actions take priority because we are in survival mode. When the amygdala fires to tell our brain that there is danger, it bypasses the frontal cortex, making it very difficult to engage in logical decision-making. This is why it is so hard to think clearly when we are under stress or in danger. When we see people who are consistently angry, we know that their brain is perceiving a threat and, therefore, are not able to use their frontal cortex. These are not the people we want in leadership because they will not be clear-headed to make logical decisions, relying only on primitive personal survival reflexes.

If the sympathetic nervous system has been activated too long or with great intensity of perceived danger, our autonomic nervous system will have exhausted its energy, and we'll collapse. This state of overwhelm leaves us exhausted with a very narrow vision of what we can do. We are unable to connect with our bodies because the sensory system is overloaded. In this state, our bodies are trying to recover. In the animal kingdom, this state might look like the bird that hit the window, lying motionless on the ground, stunned, before it eventually comes out of that state, shakes, and flies away. Humans are not as good at fully stopping or shaking it off when we are in this overwhelmed state. Even though our bodies are trying to recover, we often force ourselves to keep functioning without the resources we need. As a result, the deep recovery we need doesn't happen efficiently.

Polyvagal Theory and the Vagus Nerve

Dr. Stephen Porges declared these nervous system states the *polyvagal theory*. This theory describes the significance of the vagus nerve in relationship to the sympathetic activation system. The vagus nerve has connections to structures in the head, face, throat, chest, and digestive system. While the sympathetic nervous system is like our gas pedal, the vagus nerve is the brake. When this nerve activates, it will temper the stimulating effect of the fight-or-flight response to prevent us from becoming overwhelmed.

The vagus nerve is about 20 percent active, and 80 percent perceptive. This means that it is highly educated by messages from various places in the body to assess safety and function, both inside our body and in our environment. Most of those nerve fibres receive data from the heart and gut for our brains to respond to. This is why gut health is incredibly important in nervous system regulation.

The polyvagal theory describes the *ventral vagal* state as our place of safety. Here, the nervous system feels no threat and we are free to socially connect with others and pursue our dreams. We are aware and connected to our bodies and emotions, and we are able to attend to their needs.

Interestingly, we were not born with a fully developed ventral vagal system. This system develops in our first few months out of the womb as we make eye contact with caregivers, experience touch, and hear soothing sounds to calm ourselves. For this reason, those early months and years of life can make a huge impact on our nervous system. For those of you who are now freaking out because you didn't have a great start in life, I have good news. Thankfully, our nervous system can also heal early wounds because of neuroplasticity, simply meaning that our nervous system can learn and change.

The sympathetic nervous system activates when there are real or perceived threats. Threats might be perceived if they were once there but are no longer present. In those cases, the nervous system hasn't been updated to the fact that they no longer exist. For example, a person who was in a car accident years ago may now have symptoms of anxiety when driving that same stretch of road years later. Their nervous system hasn't updated to understand that the threat is no longer there.

The sympathetic nervous system may also be activated because the ventral vagal system was never fully developed through childhood trauma or neglect. It is the ventral vagal system that puts the brakes on the sympathetic activation system. Without a functioning brake, the system continues in chaos. Deliberately activating the vagus nerve, by using the exercises in this journey, helps to repair the braking system and restore calm in the system.

The *dorsal vagal* system causes a shutdown, overwhelm, or collapse response. We may be able to function in this state, but there is a disconnect between the body and emotions. We may feel like the walking dead. The primary function of this state is to replenish energy so we can eventually move back to a ventral vagal state. A secondary function of this state is to avoid the discomfort of the sympathetic activation that was deemed as too much. Adding more resilience will help us avoid this shutdown state.

As you journey through this process you may notice that we tend to have seasons of dominant states, but we move through these states frequently throughout the day. This is completely normal as we interact with our world.

Within the polyvagal theory, a hierarchy is described, showing the need to pass through the activated sympathetic state before we can return to a ventral calm state. This means that when we are in a season of overwhelm (dorsal vagal), we will need to activate our nervous system before we can get to the ventral vagal safety. If we are avoiding sympathetic activation because it feels dangerous, then we will not be able to get ourselves out of a dorsal vagal shutdown state. ***Activating with safety is our path to ventral vagal safety and resilience.***

Safety First

In any adventure we embark upon in life, we are prudent to think of safety first. As we learn a new skill, drive to the store, or prepare a meal: safety first. We use an oven mitt to pull a hot dish from the oven. We latch our seat belts when we get in the car. We learn safety protocols for a new sport. The same is true when it comes to our nervous system.

Many of us have limited experience with how safety feels in our nervous system. This can be especially true if we were not raised in an emotionally or physically safe environment. This is also true after physical or emotional injury.

When a person has experienced physical pain or injury resulting in some type of disability or inability, we can experience a loss of safety within our body. It becomes difficult to trust our bodies to do the tasks we need and want them to do. It becomes difficult to trust our bodies to tell us about our inner and outer worlds. This is when we learn to live in a constant state of danger rather than safety.

The problem is that our bodies do not heal well when we do not feel safe. It takes energy and resources to heal. That energy is not available to us when our inner or outer worlds do not feel safe. If you think of a wild animal in danger, all the energy they have is going toward survival. This is the *fight-or-flight* response. There is no available energy to heal when we are in the fight-or-flight state. If that sympathetic state is too intense or lasts too long, we run out of resources and we collapse into the dorsal vagal state. Active healing can't happen here either because it requires energy that is simply not there.

So, what is the solution? We need to find safety. Safety in the nervous system is stimulated through the vagus nerve. The multiple connections of the vagus nerve give us multiple ways to stimulate it, to help create an atmosphere where healing can occur.

How a Resilient Nervous System Can Help You

There are many ways that our bodies can show us that all is not well. These symptoms can either be the cause of dysfunction or the result or both.

Heart rate is an indicator of the amount of activation in our nervous system. We can feel this when we are rushing to get out of the house on time. Our heart rate increases as our nervous system activates the sympathetic nervous system to mobilize. We can then notice some time later that our heart rate has settled back down to its normal rate once the threat of being late is over. Through this journey, we will use our heart rate as one way to understand our nervous system.

Additionally, heart rate variability is shown to correlate with vagus nerve function. Heart rate variability is the slight elevation of your heart rate during the inhalation part of breath and the lowering of the heart rate when you are exhaling. This is a normal and healthy variation of our heart rate. When there is dysfunction in the vagus nerve, the heart rate variability decreases. In other words, there is less variation in the speed of your heart rate associated with breath. We want our breath and heart rate to speak to each other, speeding up the heart with inhalation and decreasing the heart rate with exhalation. Heart rate variability can be measured with a device such as a finger clip, a watch, or ring specifically designed to measure this.

We can determine the relative health of our vagus nerve by examining how easy it is to talk to someone while maintaining eye contact (while not shutting ourselves down), as well as the level of prosody (variation in pitch) in our voice. A healthy nervous system (i.e., feeling safe) means that you can maintain eye contact with others without feeling stress while staying connected to yourself. It also means that you have variation of intonation in your voice when connecting with others.

But how does it feel inside? I'm glad you asked!

When we are in a ventral vagal safety state, we are safe to connect deeply with our trusted core people or critters, and interact with others freely. We are able to have fun, laughing with abandon. We can also connect with ourselves, being a compassionate observer of our body sensations, attending to the ups and downs of the day. Our breathing is relaxed and deep. And our thoughts gravitate toward things of passion or interest.

The sympathetic state is an activated state. With safety, this might look like a workout that maintains connection to your body, or physical intimacy. In these states, we are activated but the safety we feel allows us to connect with ourselves and/or others. Without safety, it is a fight-or-flight state. Our heart rate is elevated, our muscles are tight, and we might get angry easily. In this state we are on high alert to our surroundings and attuned to danger. Our gaze tends to scan for danger as our eyes dart back and forth. We will perceive messages in our body and in our surroundings as messages of danger. If our default setting is the sympathetic state, we will have difficulty finding beauty and strength in ourselves or our surroundings.

In a dorsal vagal overwhelm state, we have lost connection with and awareness of our body. We might live mostly in our head. In this state it is difficult to get motivated and we can feel stuck in various aspects of life. Our gaze will tend to be more fixed, as opposed to scanning as in the sympathetic state or in connection with people or aspects of interest in our surroundings as we would in ventral vagal. In dorsal vagal overwhelm, we may be immobilized, unable to perform tasks we usually could, or we may perform them but with little connection to the tasks or their outcomes. We might prefer to shut the world out completely.

The goal is not to be in the ventral vagal state all the time. There are appropriate times to be in an activated state. The energy conservation properties of the dorsal vagal state provide some benefits when the tank is empty. The goal for our nervous system ought to be resilience. In other words, we want to be able to shift between states with ease.

Shifting states with ease means that we can activate our nervous system to move more quickly when deadlines demand it or when fleeing from actual danger. Shifting states with ease also means that we will be able to shift down easily at the end of the day to fall asleep when the body and mind need rest.

Resilience in our nervous system also means that we can be present with uncomfortable things, doing hard things without becoming unravelled, panicked, or shutting down. In the psychology world, they call this the *window of tolerance*.

For people who have experienced trauma, it can be very difficult to do anything in a sympathetic state without it feeling like danger, quickly pushing us into overwhelm. Let me demonstrate.

Years after a traumatic event, after receiving excellent trauma care, I found myself in an academically challenging time. I blocked off time from work to study so I could be as prepared as possible. But my family had other plans. Unexpectedly, family came to town wanting to get physiotherapy treatment, something I was usually happy to do, but this weekend was off limits. After a shaming political conversation when they already hijacked my study time, I went to bed only to be woken up with chest and neck pain. After weeks of ignoring things and pushing through, I finally felt space in my life to have things checked out (not a wise decision, by the way!). All my labs were perfect, but my EKG was not. I had a possible cardiac event, related to stress.

Months later, I committed to taking my niece and two nephews to South America. One of our adventures was to hike Machu Picchu. I needed to train because I had never hiked that long or with that level of vertical gains, or at that elevation (I live at sea level!). During this training I was acutely aware of my heart. I had to find a way to push my body without my heart running away like a downhill-careening truck with no brakes. What I realize now is that I was learning to be in a sympathetic state without it feeling dangerous. As I physically trained for the Machu Picchu hike, I increased my awareness of the signs of safety. I got an all-clear from a cardiologist to ensure that these perceptions of safety were based on reality. And I correlated physical effort with feelings of joy and connection, often hiking with friends, which helped to keep the ventral vagal system onboard. I taught my heart that it could increase its pace for a reason other than mortal danger. For a nervous system with a history of trauma, my nervous system only knew sympathetic activation because of danger. Hence, any activation, even hiking, would default to flooding my system with stress hormones, until I taught it about safety.

Know Your Window of Tolerance

The idea of a *window of tolerance* was first coined by Dr. Dan Siegel, a psychiatrist and author. He describes the window of tolerance as a range of arousal that our nervous system can manage. With too much arousal, our nervous system becomes overwhelmed, and we function less effectively. With too little arousal, our nervous system will become depressed and disconnected with present reality.

The over-aroused state can look like the fight-or-flight response of the sympathetic nervous system previously described. This might be feelings of anxiety, panic, a sense of needing to run away, or the feeling of overwhelm, or a "deer in headlights" feeling.

When we are in an under-aroused state, we may have feelings of depression, and a disconnection with ourselves. We may zone out, be clumsy, or injure ourselves because we lose a sense of where we are in space. We have difficulty connecting to what we are feeling in our body.

The depth of our window of tolerance reflects our nervous system in this moment. And it can change. The expressions of exceeding the window of tolerance will happen automatically because it is part of our autonomic nervous system. Our window of tolerance can expand or contract with the seasons of life, but we can actively expand it through deliberate exercise.

Stress and trauma are factors that will shrink our window of tolerance. This effect can be fleeting or over a long season. If we have a narrow window of tolerance, it doesn't take much to push us to a state of overwhelm. This might look like collapsing in the chair when we finally find the lost key, or losing our temper when someone looks at us angrily. A small window of tolerance can also affect the under-aroused side of the window. In a season of stress, perhaps having an evening with nothing to do leads to feelings of depression and loneliness. Maybe we keep busy to avoid uncomfortable thoughts and emotions. This can be a sign of a small window of tolerance.

The goal in working with our window of tolerance is not to stay in safely in the centre. If we do not use the space we have, we will lose the space. When we lose the depth of our window of tolerance, we become highly reactive to smaller and smaller stimuli. This might even include an increasing list of food sensitivities; where once we were able to eat a wide variety of foods, our nutritional palette becomes much smaller as our window of tolerance becomes smaller. This might also be true of our comfort with social activities, as we may have seen with the COVID-19 pandemic response. For many of us, as we saw fewer people, we could tolerate smaller groups of people, where bigger groups were easier before the pandemic. It takes effort to push a little past our comfort zone to increase our window without pushing us into a state of overwhelm.

After a season of stress or trauma, we will often find the need to expand our window of tolerance. As a physiotherapist, I see people who have had pain. By its nature, pain is stressful. So, when I see people in my clinic, their window of tolerance is smaller than it might have been before the injury, accident, or diagnosis. But creating change in a nervous system with a compressed window of tolerance is difficult because it doesn't take much therapeutic intervention for it to be "too much." So, increasing resilience, or widening our window of tolerance will allow us to receive the therapeutic interventions we need to heal.

A person with a vibrant nervous system has the capacity to race to a bus they are about to miss, or to sit with themselves in quiet rest. A person with a vibrant nervous system has the capacity to alternate between high arousal and low arousal with relative ease, without putting them into an overwhelmed state or dragging them into depression.

This journey is designed to welcome you to a greater awareness of your window of tolerance and then to gently nudge the boundaries. Because our nervous systems have the capacity to change (neuroplasticity for the win!), we can exercise our nervous system to tolerate and embrace greater arousal. This will allow us to rest more peacefully and to move and engage with greater varieties of life experiences.

Awareness Exercises for Nervous System Safety and Resilience

- **First steps:** Do you feel that you are currently within your window of tolerance? Do you feel at the top of the window, close to overstimulated, or close to the bottom, toward under-stimulation and depression? How do you know? What evidence do you have that tells you where you are? What physical sensations do you feel when you are overstimulated or under-stimulated?

  What you learn about "how you know" will help give you the guardrails and feedback to do the exercises in a neurologically safe way. So, it is helpful to be as specific as possible with the signals your body gives you about these states.

- **Next steps:** As you go through a day, take a snapshot of various times in the day, and watch how you move through your window of tolerance. What are the sensations that tell you where you are in your window? The sensations you experience might be unique to you. Some people might feel a change in their heart rate, or a tightening in their stomach as they approach the upper limits of their window. As people approach the lower limits of their window they might feel a heaviness, darkness, or sleepiness. As you notice your varying signals, try to find multiple markers along the way. You didn't immediately jump to the top or drop to the bottom of your window. You were climbing or sliding there. See if you can identify some of the signals you may have missed that are telling you that you are starting to climb up or slide down. Remember, the goal in life is not to stay directly in the middle. The goal is to have a broad width of life experiences, exploring highs and lows within your window.

➤ **Advanced steps**: Expanding your window! This is what this book is all about. Now that you are familiar with your current window, remember that as you make changes to your nervous system, the window of tolerance will also change. With trauma, the window can become narrower. With deliberate work to expand your nervous system, your window of tolerance should grow. In addition to the specific exercises in this book, simply doing new things, eating new things, or doing things differently (a different path home from work, using your non-dominant hand), will help to wake up the nervous system to allow the idea of change without triggering a threat response. These are simple, easy things that should not feel dangerous. Build an expectation of the unexpected in your nervous system.

Building Guardrails for Your Nervous System

The following exercises are your guardrails for the rest of the exercises. They will help you get the most out of the rest of the exercises and enable you to progress while avoiding an overstimulation of your nervous system. Please complete the following before continuing.

Vagus Nerve Stimulation Exercises

While all the exercises in this book are designed to engage the vagus nerve, the following two exercises are a simple starting point. They are not a magic bullet to fix everything. Doing these exercises when needed may help you progress through the other exercises with greater ease.

1. Gargle or hum. Vibration in the back of the throat helps to stimulate the vagus nerve. Gargling or humming will create that vibration. When humming, try a range of tones and see if your nervous system prefers a certain range. You might notice physical signs of relaxation such as a slower heart rate, deeper and slower breath, or the shoulders dropping into a more relaxed position.
2. Massage the ear. The ear has vagus nerve endings, making this an easy place to physically access the vagus nerve. This massage should not be painful. Massage the cartilage of the ear to find any specific spots that might feel like they need a little more softness. The left ear has a greater connection to the heart compared to the right. If you need to calm your heart rate quickly, a gentle massage of the left ear may help.

Finding Your Safe Anchors

1. Finding a "space" safety anchor: This is often the easiest anchor to think of because there is no need to tune into yourself to do it. If you have difficulty with mindfulness or feeling sensations, this is a good place to start. Think of a place that feels safe and calm to you. For me, that is the ocean. I grew up in northern Alberta, without access to the ocean. I now live twenty-five minutes away from the ocean. Every time I get to the ocean, I sigh at first glance. This is my nervous system coming into a deeper ventral vagal state. As I spend time near the ocean, my gaze consistently goes back to the water. I can do other things, focus on other tasks, but I come back to the

view of the ocean as my safe place to anchor. What is your space anchor?
2. Finding an "object" safety anchor: This anchor requires a little connection to yourself but is still an external anchor. This usually makes it a little more challenging than the space anchor but can allow us to bring a physical anchor with us. To find your safe object anchor you might consider a meaningful object or a physical sensation you enjoy touching. For example, some people choose a specific smooth stone to carry that they can pass their fingers over when they need help to come back to ventral vagal safety. Maybe you have a favourite smell or essential oil that can bring you back to ventral.
3. Finding a "part of self" safety anchor: This is the trickiest one. To find your safe anchor in self requires you to do the body scan exercise. As you do a body scan, consider what part of your body feels the safest. This might change, especially after an injury. If you've had pain, you might think that you don't have a safe body part. Every body has a safest spot. It doesn't need to be completely safe, just the safest. If you can't yet find a "safest" place in your body, try asking which part feels the strongest.

Using Your Anchors

You can use your anchors throughout the day when you realize that you have left your ventral vagal safety. Take a moment to think about the space anchor. For me, seeing the ocean and engaging as many senses as I can about the ocean — smells, sounds etc. — will help anchor me into a ventral vagal state. Focusing attention on our "part of self" anchor and physically touching that safe body part, feeling it from the inside or outside will bring us back to our body, which invites us back into a ventral vagal state.

Know Your States
Knowing what state you are in is crucial for the exercises in this book. The exercises will guide you to a greater understanding, but let's start with writing a list.
1. Write a list of physical or mental sensations you have when you are overwhelmed. How do you know that this has happened?
2. Write a list of physical or mental sensations you have when you are activated in a sympathetic fight-or-flight state.
3. Write a list of physical or mental sensations you have when you feel safe, calm, and restful.

Body Awareness
Becoming aware of your body is a first step to safe and productive movement. How body aware are you? Take a moment to connect with the inner world that is your body. Do you notice your breathing pattern, your heart rate, or your level of activation? Do you notice pressure in your body anywhere, such as whatever surface is supporting you? If you are sitting, do you feel pressure on your sit bones?

If these questions are difficult to answer, it's possible that you do not yet view your body as safe enough to connect with it. Don't worry, we will build trust gradually to deepen trust in your body and your sense of safety in it.

To build trust, you can start with a mechanical observation of the body. Rather than trying to feel your body from the inside, be an observer. For example, place your hands evenly across your lower ribs and observe the movement patterns of your rib cage as you breathe. Don't make an effort to change anything. You are only a compassionate observer of what your body is doing. There is no value statement to be made about the correct way to breathe. This is about reintroducing yourself to your body to build trust and understanding. If using rib cage movement feels too intimate for you, start with your hands on another part of the body that feels the safest to touch. Notice the sensation of touch, notice any muscle tension you feel under your hands. Remember that in the early stages, you are observing from the outside, not the inside.

Interoception

Once it feels safe to observe your body from the outside you can progress to becoming compassionately connected to the inner life of your body, from the inside. Stephen Porges calls this *interoception*. Some ideas on how to do this would be any mindfulness exercise that you might be familiar with. Ideas for increasing the interoceptive abilities of your nervous system would include the following:

Breath awareness: Feel your breathing patterns from within. Do you feel your rib cage moving in synchrony? Do you feel any other pressure in your body with inhalation or exhalation? What feels easier to do, breathing in or breathing out? Do you feel the moment when your body feels an urge to breathe in or out?

Heart rate awareness: Can you tune in to your heart rate? Do you feel the lub-dub pattern of the beat? What do you notice about the heart rate as you try to observe it? Do you notice a change in your heart rate as you think about your tasks for the day, or if you think about certain people such as challenging people or loving people?

Body scan awareness: In stillness, lying or sitting, do a body scan of compassionate observation. You can start at the head or the feet; do what feels good. Notice if you feel tension somewhere, more or less pressure on one side compared to the other. Notice where your body feels most at ease. Are your hands at ease, your knees, your nose? What is your favourite part of your body today?

Movement awareness: With the skills you have now developed to tune in to your body, you can add awareness of these elements to movement. If you are sitting, observe your breath or your heart rate as you stand up or move a limb. Did anything change? Now progress to more complicated movement patterns such as daily life movement patterns (brushing teeth, work duties, etc.): walking, running, sports. Are you able to stay connected to your body in a way to compassionately notice if the right side feels the same as the left, or to notice any movement patterns that don't feel smooth? Remember, we are not passing judgment on your body. These are not bad parts of your body. There are no bad parts.

The increase in body awareness is meant to increase our trust in our body, not to chastise and judge it. If you notice something in your body that feels restricted, please resist the temptation to let it overtake you. That is the dorsal vagal collapse state that is overwhelmed. If that happens, pause, back off the detail of your observation a little until you can observe the challenges *and* the strengths that exist in your body. When you can do that, savour those parts of the body that feel at ease and strong. This will help you stay in a ventral vagal state in your relationship with your body.

Building Safety and Resilience Through the Body

TRAVELLING THE JOURNEY OF LIFE requires a physical body. A body is necessary for life, survival, connection, and play. We use body movement to progress in health, in relationships, in careers, and in life. We also use our bodies to regulate our nervous systems.

When we are in a sympathetic activated state such as anxiety, we feel an intense urge to move. We use phrases like "burn some energy" and may describe our inner state as vibrating or buzzing. The need for movement becomes very intense in the sympathetic state. But what happens when we have a condition, an injury, or a pain pattern that makes movement difficult or impossible? Or what if we are in a state of dorsal vagal shutdown and movement feels impossible even though it is technically possible?

The hierarchy of the nervous system states dictates that we must pass through the sympathetic (movement) state to get ourselves out of the dorsal vagal overwhelm and back to a place of safety where our whole beings can heal well (physically, mentally, emotionally, spiritually, and relationally). When the immobilization of the dorsal vagal state is intense, such as with trauma or with a prolonged time in an activated state, mobilization can be very difficult, but not impossible. The first step exercises are designed for exactly that purpose, to get our system familiar with safety in movement, by being connected to our bodies. Much like strengthening a weak muscle, you cannot start lifting 100 lb weights when you can now only lift your arm. So, we start with what we are able to do now, which will give us more strength in our nervous system to do even more.

Mindfulness

The concept of mindfulness is not a new one. However, there has been an increased focus on mindfulness recently. So, what is it? Essentially, mindfulness is the process of increasing awareness. Mindfulness of our physical sensations from outside our body can involve simply increasing our awareness of the sights and smells around us, or feeling the sensations on our body such as pressure when we push on a body part. Mindfulness also involves increasing our awareness of the inner workings of our body. This can include an awareness of breath, heart rate, or any physical sensations of emotions.

Mindfulness has been shown to increase greater resilience or regulation in our nervous systems. By becoming aware of the messages our body is sending us, we can respect the needs our body has. This will allow us to pause when we need to, to decrease the intensity of an activity because we are on the verge of an injury, or to let go of hesitation when we are safe to be fully in a joyous moment or in the process of overcoming obstacles.

The practice of mindfulness can be tricky for those who have had PTSD or have had some level of dissociation from their body, such as with complex chronic pain. In these situations, the body has become an unsafe place, and the first goal would be to establish a safe relationship with the body. We do this by changing the neural pathways between the brain and the body. This is the goal of mindfulness. By increasing awareness of our responses, we can change those responses, giving the system other options. This also helps to increase trust in our body as we begin to receive more reliable messages about its movement, its impulses, and its safety.

If you have a history of out-of-body dissociation, please speak with your mental health provider about any concerns with starting a mindfulness-based program, as some of these exercises may not be appropriate for you.

The progression of exercises in this book relies heavily on an ability to read your body signals telling you which nervous system state you are in. The prompts used assume that you can read your inner body sensations to tell you when an exercise is too much or when it is safe and helpful to proceed to another level. Therefore, it is important to practise the safety steps from the earlier chapter and this mindfulness section to be clear about your window of tolerance. It may seem redundant and very basic, but you are rewiring your brain to establish a line of communication so your body can tell you when it feels safe. We want to strengthen and reinforce your nervous system's pattern to safely push the edges, rather than reinforce a dysregulating pattern of activation or overwhelm. To do that we must know the edges of our window of tolerance.

A central element to the practice of mindfulness is that it is a non-judgmental and compassionate awareness of our body. We are taught by society to judge ourselves, and the advertising world is built upon us feeling not good enough so they can sell us something. In mindfulness, we let go of any moral judgment about ourselves. Noticing a greater expansion of our breath on one side compared to another is not a fault. It is communication. It might be our body telling us that it wants some attention somewhere. A high heart rate is not a "bad" thing. It is a message to tell us that our nervous system perceives danger. It is then up to us to assess if the danger is real or if it is a leftover message that has not been updated to a safer, current reality.

Mindfulness Exercises for Nervous System Safety and Resilience

➤ **First steps**: In whatever position you are currently in, notice the contact of the surface that is holding you up. If you are standing, feel your feet on the floor. If you are sitting, feel the seat pushing back at you, holding you up. If these positions already flood your system with messages of pain, find a position where you feel the least amount of physical pain. Then shift your focus from the inner messages of pain that your nervous system is receiving and feel the sensation of your supporting surface pushing back at you, and shift to a perspective of gratitude for the surface holding you. Notice as specifically as you can, where this surface contacts your body. How much pressure do you feel? What does it feel like if you take the pressure off? Do you notice any change as you shift to a perspective of gratitude?

As you do this exercise of awareness, do you have a sense of it feeling safe to observe this pressure? If it does, you can expand the exercise by adding pressure in other places and simply feeling the pressure. Use your own body to add pressure to other parts of your body so you are in full control of the pressure to maintain a sense of safety. Try pushing your finger, thumb, hand, heel, or whatever body part into another, with some gentleness at first. Vary your pressure and/or your speed as well as changing locations. Remember that you are still trying to stay in the zone of safety for your body, but you are also trying to remind your body that not every touch is a painful and dangerous touch. You are teaching your brain to know the difference.

Next steps: Once you feel comfortable with increased awareness of physical sensation from the outside, then we can progress to mindfulness from the inside. This means that you are feeling sensations from within your body. If you are comfortable with anatomy and are a visual person, it might be helpful to look at images of body anatomy as you do the next steps.

To bridge the gap between outside and inside observation, we can assess the heart rate. You can start by placing your fingers as you would if you were taking your pulse. The two easiest places to do this are at the neck and at your wrist. At the neck, you will find your carotid pulse just under your chin on either side, just in front of the muscle that goes from the ear to the top of the breastbone. At the wrist, you will find your radial pulse on the inside surface of your wrist, just at the bendy part, at the base of your thumb. If you think you are in the right spot but don't feel a pulse, lighten your fingers a bit.

Once you have found your pulse, feel the pulse pounding on your fingertips. Feel the rhythm of it. Then, shift inside your own body to see if you can feel it from there. It may be helpful to have a hand on your breastbone to help you connect to your heart.

When you can notice your heart rate from inside, try thinking of something or someone who is a little stressful to you. Only a little stressful. What do you notice about your heart rate? Now, think about something or someone who is safe, comfortable, and affirming to you, and again, notice your heart rate.

The goal with this exercise is to notice sensations in your body without assigning worth or value, without determining their goodness or badness, and then to notice changes in those sensations. These sensations are the language your body uses to tell you how calm or stressed you are. You will rely on these messages to keep you within your window of tolerance.

➤ **Advanced steps:** Once you can safely connect with your outside body and with an element of your inside body, then it is time to notice the whole body from inside. You will start with the body scan. In whatever position you are in, start by noticing your body from the inside. Work systematically in a way that makes sense to you. Notice differences between the right and left sides. Notice the places that feel good as well as those that don't (we often are geared to noticing the parts that feel bad). Notice parts that feel soft or firm, hot or cold. This is an observation without judgment. It is a way for you to reintroduce yourself to your body and allow your body to communicate to you. What parts are begging for attention? What parts have you not noticed in awhile? You can zoom in your awareness to include specific parts like a strong-feeling finger or a dull and unaware eyebrow, for example. You can also zoom out your awareness and make observations about your whole self as a unit.

Breathing

Breathing is helpful for life, health, and happiness. In fact, it is necessary. Adults breathe an average of twelve to twenty times a minute, which is roughly 25,000 times a day, or 8.5 million times a year. How we breathe affects our health and our sense of well-being. Our breath is deeply connected to our nervous system.

One of the ways that our nervous system tells us that it is stressed or that we are under threat is by breathing more shallow and rapid, as it prepares to fight or flee.

This nervous system connection is also shown on a micro level in something called *heart rate variability* (HRV), as mentioned in the previous chapter. During inhalation, our heart rate speeds up a little, and it slows slightly when we breathe out. A nervous system that has had trauma or chronic stress loses the variability in the heart rate, low HRV. If you already have a wearable device that can measure HRV, you can monitor progress in your nervous system as you complete the exercises in this book.

The breath of life is the process where we bring oxygen into our bodies. But equally important is the removal of the carbon dioxide we produce with metabolism. The exhalation is, therefore, as important as the inhalation.

Effective breathing has three components of movement: the belly, the lower rib cage, and the upper rib cage. The lower part of our lung is our most efficient part for receiving oxygen. This means that belly and lower rib cage breathing is the most effective. Relying on only the upper rib cage will result in a feeling of not enough air. This feeling often correlates with a sense of panic. This is not the nervous system we want to activate in most situations. The top rib cage (or shoulders/traps) can be used in a deep inhale to get that last little bit of air when we need "extra," not in a normal resting breath. In a fight-or-flight situation with actual danger, we will need a lot of oxygen to run or fight. This is the time that this breathing pattern is added to the deep lower lung breaths. The upper rib cage breathing pattern should not be activated in a normal resting situation.

When we breathe in, our bellies should expand outwards in all directions. However, a healthy pattern will also see some lower rib expansion as this happens. Focusing only on the movement of the belly can lead people to push their belly out using the pressure of the air in their lungs, by slightly holding their breath and bearing down. This can cause problems in the pelvic floor or in the abdomen by creating weakness, resulting in hernias. That pressure will also activate our nervous system, preventing us from getting into a true ventral vagal safety state. In that pattern, we are trying too hard to be restful. We should be invited into rest rather than pushing ourselves there.

Breathing Exercises for Nervous System Safety and Resilience

- **First step:** In a quiet place, gently notice your breathing patterns. Notice the pattern of your belly when you breathe in and out. Does it rise when you inhale and fall when you exhale? Do your ribs expand outwards with your breath? Place your hands on your lower rib cage on the sides, where the side seam of your shirt would be. Do you feel your hands separate from each other, expanding outwards as you breathe in, and coming closer to each other when you breathe out? And lastly, do you feel your breastbone lift when you breathe in? As you notice your natural breathing patterns, take a slightly deeper breath. Does your pattern of breathing change? When taking a slightly deeper breath, try to expand your belly first, then your ribs and then your breastbone only at the end. Practise this same pattern in your normal breath.

- **Next steps:** Once the belly-rib-breastbone pattern of breathing feels a bit more natural to you, bring your attention to the in-out rhythm of your breathing. Do you spend more time inhaling or exhaling? Because the nervous system is meant to activate a little with each inhale, and calm a little when we exhale, see if you can notice a bit of an awake feeling when you breathe in compared to when you breathe out. To help strengthen your nervous system we will exaggerate this a little bit by speeding up the inhalation and slowing down the exhalation. We often think that breathing in is the most important part of the breath and put our focus on it. But an efficient exhale will increase overall health and will stimulate the ventral vagal safety nervous system. Try a slightly quicker inhale and then a prolonged exhale. Blowing your air out through a pursed lip will help you lengthen the exhale and will create the vibration that can stimulate the vagus nerve, giving you an even greater calming effect. It is not holding your breath; we want a constant and slow exhale. If you are in dorsal vagal overwhelm, you will need to activate your nervous system to get back to ventral vagal. To do this, take a few (only a few) quick inhale breaths, with a normal exhale. Do you feel how energizing that is? When you need energy, take a few quick inhale breaths; but if you need calm, a few long exhale breaths. Each of these exercises are meant to be exercises, not corrective breathing patterns, so after a couple of repetitions, return to your normal resting breathing pattern, the one that requires no effort or thought. Notice any changes in your nervous system.

Advanced steps: As you will discover in the posture section later in the book, our nervous system activates when we arch our rib cage back, pointing our breastbone to the sky (not arching from the low back!). And we calm our nervous system with a soft curved spine. Let's bring that into a breathing exercise to help reinforce our nervous system so it can transition from calm to activation to calm. Standing, sitting, or in any posture, practise the rhythmic breathing from the previous exercise. As you breathe in, arch your upper back a little, pointing your breastbone upward. As you breathe out, drop your breastbone down a little, letting your upper back return to its resting state. What do you notice in your nervous system as you do that? If your nervous system feels okay with this, try a little more movement. Maybe you want to fully curl in when you exhale and fully arch your mid-back as you inhale. Try to do these exercises in a state of awareness of what your body is feeling. If you notice that you are only going through the motions, not tuned in to your body, or only able to observe from the outside, do a smaller movement. If it still feels good to do a larger movement and you can stay connected to your body, consider adding more body parts. Perhaps your arms or legs curl in when you exhale and spread like a star when you inhale. Notice what this feels like in your body. Savour any empowering sensations you might be having as you do these breathing exercises.

Body Movement

Movement is how we exist in the world, in our environment, and how we get things done. But movement is also needed to bring us to health. Movement is needed for physiological health, digestive health, as well as mental and emotional health. We use movement to connect or disconnect with people and we use movement to express and embody our deep mental, emotional, and spiritual selves. Movement is important!

As mentioned previously, movement is necessary to bring us out of a dorsal vagal shutdown/overwhelm to a place of safety. If we are in a dorsal vagal shutdown state and need to mobilize to do a task, we may feel unable to do this. If we are in a fight-or-flight activated state, we may not be compassionately connected to our body to allow movement in all available zones of the body.

When we move, we remind our bodies that they have the capacity to defend themselves and stay safe on a cellular level.

This brings us back to safety. The exercises provided might seem basic and entirely too simple if you are used to running marathons. However, the goal is to move with awareness. Athletes are often trained to ignore messages from the body, override them, to win. This can cause injury, which eventually pays a toll. But we want to win in life. So, we want to increase our awareness as we move, so we can move safely through this journey of life.

An essential component of movement is cardiovascular fitness. Using cardio as a weight loss tool may or may not be effective. In short, we will not lose weight sustainably if we are in a fight-or-flight survival mode. In that state, our body secretes hormones that hold fat to be used later and that secretes its own hormones, further challenging our health. Intense cardio workouts that push you into a danger state will not yield weight loss results. Heart health is a more important reason to do cardiovascular exercise. Our heart is a mirror of our nervous system. If we never move in a way that increases our heart rate, we significantly decrease our nervous system resilience and strength. It is important to get our heart rate up through daily movement. How we do this is important. Choosing exercise that is fun, while keeping compassionately connected to your body, will help build nervous system safety and resilience.

Movement Exercises for Nervous System Safety and Resilience

- **First steps:** If you have a moment, day, or week of feeling overwhelmed and immobilized, it might feel unrealistic to your nervous system to go to the gym or go for a run, even though movement is needed to get you out of that state. If this is the case, try to move a body part. It could be making a fist or tapping a foot. As you do this, tune in to your nervous system, and notice how you feel a little more energized, like the suggestion to do a workout might not be as unreasonable as it did before you moved a small body part.

Do the same movement, or something different, but now pick up the speed a little. If you are still within your window of tolerance, if it doesn't feel overwhelming, pick up the speed a little more. You can take a break if you need to, and then repeat this until you feel less overwhelmed at the thought of movement. This is not overriding your body telling you to rest. If you need to rest, you will feel the energizing part of the nervous system activate and then a feeling of being tired; whereas an overwhelmed system will respond to activation with some degree of dissociation, where your connection with your body is lost. It is important to know the difference between feeling tired and feeling overwhelmed and disconnected from your body. An overwhelmed nervous system needs safe activation while being tired needs rest.

It is possible that your nervous system has registered every overwhelm message as fatigue. If you can't distinguish between the feeling of overwhelm and that of fatigue, practise some mindfulness when you are on the verge of sleep. Try to notice your physical sensations of the tiredness that craves sleep. Then compare this to sensations you might feel as you think about something that might be overwhelming. Pick something that is not highly emotional. It could be that stack of papers, or dishes in the sink. Something you are avoiding doing. How are those sensations different from the pre-sleep sensations? How are they similar? This teaches your nervous system the difference between fatigue and overwhelm.

➤ **Next steps:** As you become more aware of your nervous system states, deliberately use movement within your physical and medical capabilities, to gently invite a way out of a state of dorsal vagal overwhelm. This might mean doing pelvic tilts or arm movement in your office chair after an emotionally charged phone call. Or it could be a run after overstimulation from shopping in the mall in December. Begin taking note of the days that have more sympathetic or dorsal tone to them. Once you get a sense of the day-to-day variations, consider the moment-to-moment variations in your nervous system, and invite an appropriate movement to help you manage your nervous system during those times. Seeing these regulation opportunities in the moment allows your nervous system to shift in and out of the state more frequently, and thus, with more ease.

As you become more aware of your need and desire to move, observe the body parts you choose to move. Which body parts have you not yet thought of moving? What happens in your nervous system if you try to move those parts?

If you tend to gravitate toward a sympathetic activation state, you may have a rigid rib cage. This is a normal anatomical response to an activated sympathetic nervous system because the sympathetic nerves exit the spine at the level of the rib cage. To create greater ease in the sympathetic nervous system, we need to keep the rib cage flexible. This is more than stretching or deep breathing. This requires movement in multiple directions. Consider the movements in Latin dance or belly dancing. Watch some dancers, live or on video. Notice the independence of movement in the segments of the rib cage. Try some of these same movements, without forcing the movement, start small and fluid, but try the movement in all possible directions. You may find it helpful to do this to music that you love. You should not be stretching anything or feeling the end of possible movement in any direction. It should feel smooth and fluid. Make sure that you are not holding your breath to ensure that the ribs are not rigid on the spine. As you do a little of this every day, you may notice that you are not as beholden to your sympathetic nervous system as you once were. For example, you may still become angry, but it will dissipate easier.

- **Advanced steps:** The goal with the advanced steps here is to let your nervous system guide your workouts. For example, if you are going for a walk, tune in to your nervous system to check to see if this is the right pace. Notice that we are not checking with your brain, your walking buddy, or your footwear. We are checking with your nervous system. If you find you can't connect with your body or nervous system on that mindful level while you are walking, you have probably overstimulated already. Slow it down, consider walking on your own a few times so you are not distracted by conversations as you get to know the messages of your nervous system while your body is in motion. As you tune in, notice how your nervous system tells you it wants a slower pace or a faster pace. Do you feel the signs of threat that tell you that you need to slow down? Or do you feel the nudge that is inviting more? If it doesn't immediately tell you, imagine what a faster pace would feel like in your nervous system (again, not your body/joints, but your nervous system). As you imagined that, did your inner self get excited with anticipation or drop into dread? I want you to do your workouts within your window of tolerance; not too much, not too little, but occasionally nudging the edge. Play with this awareness until you learn the nuances of the language of your nervous system in motion.

Stretching

Stretching is an important part of any physical health program. The primary purpose of stretching is not simply to lengthen something that is structurally or functionally shortened. The purpose of stretching is to hydrate, lubricate, and soften the tissues, and sometimes to lengthen. As we stretch, we encourage normal cellular fluid to be pulled into layers of tissue to allow freedom of movement. Stretching also promotes a more supple tissue by gently breaking down restrictive fibres in the tissue itself. This makes the tissue more efficient. For example, a muscle that is regularly, respectfully stretched, will be more efficient in contraction and relaxation because it will be free from surrounding restrictions, as well as being more efficient in the contractile fibres themselves.

Did you notice I said respectful stretching? What does that mean? We can do harm by stretching tissue disrespectfully. This happens when we are not tuned in to our body and the limits it expresses. This happens when we declare war on those parts that feel tight to us. When we are in pain, we can become too desperate, and utterly unkind to the tissue we are stretching. The problem with this approach is that all living tissue has survival as a top priority. By declaring war on a tight muscle, we increase the likelihood that the muscle will respond with more protective contraction, and thus, become tighter. This increases our frustration and suffering, increasing our desperation so we try even harder to get that muscle to relax! Round and round the cycle we go. We've all been there. No really, we *all* have been there!!

Mindfulness stretching is a respectful form of stretching. It has been scientifically shown to be as effective at improving freedom of movement as typical stretching, while having the added benefit of decreasing anxiety and depression. That happens because it changes your nervous system. Mindfulness stretching requires us to be reasonably aware of the inner workings of our body while we move into the position of stretch.

Stretching Exercises for Nervous System Safety and Resilience

- **First steps:** To get used to the idea of mindfulness stretching, find a body part that seems tight, but does not create pain. Move that joint to the end of its available movement and notice what the sensation is. Now back off, and try it once more, slowly, trying to see if there was a first hint of restriction that may have been missed. This might feel like the first sensation of restriction even if it isn't the actual end of available movement. If you stop at that point, do you notice any sensation? Is there any increase in heart rate or change in breathing patterns that might suggest that your body is preparing to protect itself? If you pause at that point and sense your body's hesitation, what happens? Does it relax that first level of tension to give you more ease into the next deeper tension? Did your body realize it wasn't dangerous to move in that direction? Did another body part guard itself in solidarity with the stretching part? If so, what might that body part tell you about the true source of tension in the stretching part? Is it reacting to something else completely, trying to protect a different vulnerable part?

- **Next steps:** Repeat the same process as the first steps but with a body part that has historically produced pain. Notice if your body communicated pain before tension or tension before pain. If you slow down and find that first resistance, does the level of pain change? If you have had pain for some time, your brain may have become accustomed to interpreting all sensation as pain, resulting in a defensive mechanism to avoid pain. Challenge the brain to distinguish the difference between pain and tension. This can be very difficult, but you are creating new information pathways for the brain to use.

As you do your stretch, feel the tension, and invite your nervous system to a ventral vagal place of safety using your anchors from the first chapter to feel the physical sensation of safety in your body. See if there is any shift or change that needs to occur in your mind or your body to allow a greater sense of safety while still being engaged with the tension you found. This could be shifting your breathing pattern or shifting your weight a little. The goal is not to avoid feeling tension. Tension is an indication of a limit, appropriate or inappropriate. In other words, we are not meant to move indefinitely in all directions in every joint. We have some natural limits. But tension in areas where we were meant to have movement should be embraced as it is a guide to bring us to more freedom of movement. Knowing this, the sensation of tension alone may not need to be interpreted as dangerous by your nervous system. Thank the tension for showing us where there is an issue and see if it is willing to let go of the protective pattern it may have.

Advanced steps: Stretching our body should be a daily experience for everyone who has a body. During your daily stretching time, increase your mindfulness by letting your body decide what needs to be stretched that day and for how long. Following a class or program might give you ideas on what to stretch and how. But once you have this basic stretching vocabulary established, invite your body to direct your daily stretching routine. Start by doing some body awareness exercises as previously described. Which body part feels less supple or tight? In what direction does it crave more movement? Go into a stretch for that body part. Rather than stretch a tissue for ten seconds or thirty seconds, stay tuned to your body, staying within your window of tolerance, pulling back the intensity if you notice your sympathetic nervous system becoming activated. Invite the tight tissue to melt away. Before moving to the next stretch, take a moment to repeat the movement in and out of the stretch using all the new movement. This helps create new pathways in the brain, so it understands how to use that movement in everyday life without activating a danger message. This leads to a less restricted life with less pain and suffering.

Strengthening

Real or perceived loss of strength is both debilitating and unnerving because we lose our ability to function as we'd like to. It doesn't take much time to lose strength, often catching us by surprise. It takes days, not months, to lose strength. When we lose strength, we quickly adapt to find other ways to accomplish a task. As those compensations happen, we become less aware of the original weakness.

When we are predominantly in a state of ventral vagal safety, we can safely connect to our body, and quickly become aware of weaknesses when it develops. We will have a safe relationship with our body, which can then strengthen the area of weakness with little to no inner resistance.

When we are predominantly in the fight-or-flight sympathetic state, it is difficult to slow down enough to notice a weakness develop. We are more likely to have layers of compensation patterns develop before we realize that weakness exists. Once aware of the weakness, someone frequently in a sympathetic state might quickly attack the problem with an aggressive workout routine with a higher chance of injury because the awareness of body limitations due to weakness is diminished. This also means that by the time we notice the weakness, it might feel like an insurmountable feat to undo the layers of compensation patterns, which may push us into an overwhelmed dorsal vagal state.

When we are predominantly in an overwhelmed dorsal vagal state, our view of weakness might be either a lack of awareness, denial, or a submission to the weakness. Rather than seeing a way through, we simply resign ourselves to a view that we can't do it. Our movement through space and relationships becomes dominated by an assessment of our ability to do tasks. Because we easily submit to the weakness, we may not be actively strengthening parts that are weak. This results in an even greater loss of strength and a constant diminishing of life activities. The energy it takes to pull out of this state feels insurmountable.

To review, to get out of the dorsal vagal overwhelm state requires movement, any kind of movement, however small. In contrast, to get out of sympathetic activation state, we must reconnect with our bodies.

In our strengthening routine we must stay within our window of tolerance for our nervous system, while also being sensible on a gradual increase in strengthening intensity. If we move into a sympathetic fight-or-flight system to lift a weight, it is too much, and we are more likely to injure ourselves. Staying within our window of tolerance while we nudge our body to greater strength will be much more efficient than pushing ourselves out of our window of tolerance.

Strengthening Exercises for Nervous System Safety and Resilience

➤ **First steps:** With awareness, move a body part, exploring all the directions it is meant to move. Do this without force but with deliberate awareness. Now, add some resistance. Push into something. Feel the muscle contract and then relax. If it is an easy reach, place a hand on the muscle that is working and do the push again. Feel the muscle thicken as it contracts, and then flatten as it relaxes. Notice what your nervous system feels like when it pushes into something. Does it create some fear or anxiety? Does it feel empowering? If you are in a dorsal vagal state, activating a muscle, even in a small body part, can be the window you need to get out of a dorsal vagal overwhelm.

Resist the temptation to view the muscle as all on or all off. Try to find that level of resistance where you first feel a muscle twitch. When you get to the stage of strengthening a muscle that has been very weak for an extended time, you will need to be able to identify this moment of first muscle twitch to tell you that you are doing the work even if the muscle is still too weak to move or to push or lift something. Appreciate that first twitch of muscle contraction and the new neural pathways it creates as your brain remembers movement there. Try the same awareness for a muscle that is stronger, increasing your awareness of the strength that it has.

➤ **Next steps:** Adding to the first step of pushing into something to activate a muscle, you can further strengthen the sympathetic nervous system by adding vocalization to a strengthening regime. I do not mean the holding breath grunt you often hear from the back corner of the gym. You can perform a power move such as a lunge or squat, add arms in whatever power move you'd like, and then add a warrior cry. Observe your nervous system activate with anticipation and the primal memory of a deep strength you have within. You may feel strange at first, but this activity can be a powerful emotional healing tool on its own, as well as a strengthening exercise for your muscles. And yes, you lose some of the power of this activity if you do not do the vocalization. The vibration in the throat engages the vagus nerve to help create a more resilient nervous system. The deeper warrior grunts will create more vibration and have a deeper healing effect. Try this with different warrior cries to see what your nervous system likes best today, knowing that on another day it might prefer something else.

Advanced steps: As you become more comfortable vocalizing with power moves in your strengthening routine, consider options for strengthening that have a different energy than you might normally expend. For example, lifting free weights can easily activate the sympathetic nervous system, which is totally appropriate in that situation. But Pilates, while also a strength training program, does not activate the sympathetic nervous system as much as free weights or a HIIT workout. Consider the needs of your nervous system rather than mindlessly going to your default strengthening routine. If you've had a high-pace and stressful day, you may regulate better by doing some slower Pilates exercises rather than flooding your nervous system with even more sympathetic activation by lifting weights. If you've had a sad day, verging on depression, perhaps lifting weights will help give you the energy boost in your nervous system to help keep you out of a deep depression. Learn to read your nervous system; be mindful of your strength training choices to allow greater regulation of your nervous system.

Balance and Proprioception

Proprioception is the awareness of where you are in space. Practically speaking, this is your ability to balance, or coordinate movement. The expression of proprioception can be affected by the posture you hold and by weakness you might have in your body. Proprioception can be negatively affected by tissue injury and immobility.

Proprioception is the information highway between your body and your brain. When we lose the ability to send messages from a body part, the brain will not be as detailed about the information it gathers from that area. When we protect a joint, for fear of pain, or fear of doing further damage, all the cells that detect movement become lazy. After a short time of not receiving messages from an area, the brain essentially loses interest and is less able to navigate that joint through space because it hasn't been getting the information it needs. This can cause greater hesitation for movement because we feel unsteady or uncoordinated and can cause injury.

When in ventral vagal, an injury happens but we can stay connected to the place of injury, immobilize it if needed for appropriate healing, and then easily transition to a stage of healing where movement and resistance is necessary to restore function.

In sympathetic activation, the same injury happens, but we panic. Perhaps we start by throwing every possible form of treatment at it, even when some treatments cancel each other out. We are aggressive in our rehab, often causing more tissue damage because we push too hard, causing even more tissue damage because we are not connected to our bodies. This unsafe state does not allow the body to restore the communication with the injured part, and it is more likely to be injured again because proprioception has not been restored. We can view this as trying to restore communication with an old friend. If that friend betrayed us, we don't feel safe, and communication is difficult. We must re-establish communication and safety first.

In dorsal vagal overwhelm, the injury happens, and we stop everything. We guard the injured area, and we don't believe the medical professionals when they say that it is safe to start movement. When you attempt to start movement or put weight through a joint, you feel a wave of panic and you can't make yourself do it. You feel safer if you don't move that area or don't use that joint, so you just stop using it, causing more problems.

Understanding what is happening in your nervous system at this phase of healing ensures that your life will not become smaller and smaller. Establishing a safe pathway to restore proprioception will restore trust in your body's ability to move through space, allowing you to pursue goals, explore the world, be in relationships, and be creative in play.

Balance and Proprioception Exercises for Nervous System Safety and Resilience

- **First steps:** Sitting or lying down comfortably, do a quick body scan. I don't want the "quick" to be rushed, but rather a bird's-eye glance. Ask yourself, is there a part of your body that is a bit blank, or blurry, harder to describe, compared to the other parts? This might be an area of lower proprioception. Allow the bird to fly in closer to take a closer compassionate "look" at that area. What do you notice? Do you notice more detail, or did you notice your heart rate increase and did it become even more blurry? If it became blurrier, back away a little and consider doing some other ventral vagal strengthening exercises to increase your window of tolerance and then come back and try it again. When you focus in closer and get more details, try moving that area of your body, noticing how it feels, notice the patterns of movement you are creating. You are building new communication pathways to the brain. The actual movement is not important, the communication you are creating is the goal of this exercise.

Try adding new sensations to your movement. This can be walking barefoot on grass or sand. Or sitting on a different surface such as a large yoga ball. This wakes up the communication pathways between your brain and the body part that is connecting with the earth. Nature walks, earthing, or grounding can be helpful to increase your awareness of your connection to the earth.

Next steps: Start to increase your awareness of your body as you sway side to side, forward and back. Increase your awareness as you shift your weight from one leg to the other if you are standing, sit bones if you are sitting. Now fully lift one leg off the ground and then the other. Increase the difficulty of the movements you choose until you have gone through all imaginable positions you currently use in life or that you realistically want to be using in your life. Do all of this with mindfulness, increasing your awareness of the movement, how it feels in your body, and how your nervous system responds. Be aware of your window of tolerance as you do this, being careful to stay within your window. The goal is to practise being tuned in to your body in a wide variety of positions. You are encouraging your brain to become more aware of the movement, weight transfers, and joint pressures in places that might have diminished proprioception.

Advanced steps: You will now challenge your balance and proprioception further, to notice glitches in your movement patterns. These glitches may give you clues about a protective or avoidant pattern you have in your body. When this happens, your nervous system will move into an activated state, even just for a second or less. This activation tells your body that it isn't safe to move in that way and you can make slight adjustments to avoid it. The goal of this exercise is to find those spots and attend to them so they can be re-educated to a place of safety. This does not include movements of pain as described in the movement section. These are pain-free movements that may still activate your nervous system.

Pick a movement pattern that feels a bit awkward or clumsy to you. Now, do that movement much slower than you normally would. As you do, you may find a spot that feels off balance or glitchy, not smooth. At this point, find your limit of proprioception by staying within that body-connected ventral vagal state, edging slightly to that place where you are about to lose connection with your body. Do you notice any clues about the source of danger that is sending you out of your window of tolerance? If this is fear, fear of what?

Once you identify the place of the danger, even very slight, ask yourself and your nervous system if the fear is real or imagined. The tissues have a memory. If there was a time when there was danger in that position or in that movement, that fear may hijack the proprioceptive messages from that body part. Thank the body part for showing you this. This often has a sense of being on holy ground. You may or may not know what this danger or threat was. It could be a physical threat or an emotional threat. When it came up doing this exercise, you may have had a memory flash about the event. We do not need to cognitively understand it and its source. We feel it in our bodies, which indicates that we can help that piece heal using the body. Often simply seeing the component of the movement pattern will be enough to release the physiological impact of that threat. If that is the case, you can try the exact same movement again. With an awareness of the source of that moment of threat, do you have the same response, or has it dissipated? This may need a few rounds and if this is a very strong sensation of threat, it may require a somatic-based trauma counsellor to help work through the significance of that movement pattern.

Posture

The posture you hold reveals a lot about you, both in your structure and in the internal state of your nervous system. We might recognize someone who has depression by their slumped posture or characterize someone as full of themselves based on their puffed-up chest. All this without hearing a word they say, only by their posture.

As previously described, our nervous system has sympathetic and parasympathetic nerves. The activating sympathetic nerves leave your spine at your rib cage level, from the bottom of the neck to the squishy part of the abdomen. These nerves connect with each other along the right and left side of your spine. When you arch back with your rib cage, you stretch this pathway. When you slump, you give them more space.

The vagus nerve and other parts of the parasympathetic nervous system come from the brain stem and neck, as well as the lower back and pelvis. This vagus nerve acts as a brake to the sympathetic activation. When we stand or sit in a position where our head is thrust forward, we compress the neck and the pathway of the vagus nerve. Furthermore, because the vagus nerve is associated with safety, we must have freedom to scan our environment to look for signs of danger. A tightly held neck does not permit the nervous system to scan the environment to declare it to be safe. We need neck mobility to experience the safety of ventral vagal with ease. Our posture plays a huge role in neck movement.

An important function of posture is its ability to move in and out of various positions to accomplish tasks. In many cases, we are taught or shown the "correct" posture, then we try to hold that posture as long as humanly possible. This does not serve our bodies or our lives. The goal with good posture is that it is anatomically held upright while maintaining as much ease of movement as possible.

Good posture can be found primarily with the position of our pelvis or sit bones. Our resting posture should include our sit bones pointing downward, not tucked in under us. If we try to correct bad posture by pulling the shoulders back, we are working way too hard, which pushes our nervous system into sympathetic activation. Good posture should be easy, but not lazy.

Posture Exercises for Nervous System Safety and Resilience

- **First steps:** While standing or sitting, connect with your nervous system. Try to assess your level of activation. Move in and out of a slight slump. This should not be a huge movement and is *not* a stretch! As you tune in to your nervous system, do you notice a difference when you are slumped versus with the breastbone lifted? If you started this exercise in more of a dorsal state, do you feel that you are a little more awake and alert when you point your breastbone upwards? If you started this exercise in sympathetic activation, do you feel how you become a little more relaxed when you slightly slump your rib cage?

Try the same awareness exercise with neck movement. Do you feel a difference in your nervous system if you jut your head forward? How about if you press your chin back into your throat? Now try to find the space between those two options that has the most ease, the most options for movement. You have now found your neck home base.

Next steps: Sitting with your feet on the floor, rock your pelvis back and forth, tucking your tailbone under and sticking your tailbone out. Do you notice when your sit bones make the best contact with your sitting surface? The sit bones are the boney points under each buttock, not your tailbone. Notice the difference in your nervous system as you do the pelvic tilts. You will notice that this affects the rib cage position as well as the neck position. When you have that place of best sit bone contact, you will have the home base for your spine, which holds your nervous system.

As you bring your awareness to your sit bones, shift your weight from side to side and notice if you feel them both evenly. As you shift, be sure to not push into one side or the other. Just shift your body side to side. Try to find that midpoint where you can feel both sides equally. When you settle into that spot, what does the rest of your body feel like? Is it easier or harder to invite ease into other parts of your body? Is it easier or harder to reach for something or to twist when you start in that home base? Is it easier or harder to move your neck to look side to side? If you have difficulty getting them even, you may need to contact your manual therapist to address mechanical asymmetry in your pelvic bones.

➤ **Advanced steps:** With compassionate body awareness, put yourself in various positions you use regularly in your life. This could be standing, sitting, various positions for sport or play, or while washing dishes or vacuuming. As you are in these postures, do you notice where there is tension and where there is ease? Try moving in and out of those postures in a variety of directions. These will be fairly small movements, reflective of real-life movement, not stretching your body to its limits. What do you notice as you move in and out of the postures?

If you notice a movement pattern that is not smooth, try to identify the place that the movement jumps, where it isn't smooth. Is there a place your body can't go? Is something tight? Is something painful and you have a guarding response? If so, slow the movement down even more so you approach the thing your body is guarding but you don't activate the guarding response. What do you notice about the thing it is guarding? Is it a real threat of pain or instability? Is this something you will want to stretch to give more freedom of movement? Is this a weak muscle that you want to take some time to wake up and strengthen to provide more balance to the movement?

As you move in and out of a posture, do you notice an increase in tension in other parts of your body? Is there an area that feels like it is working hard to make that transition? If so, start by inviting that area to find a place of ease. For example, did your shoulders go up toward your ears as you reach away from your body? If so, invite your shoulder to drop into an easier posture as you reach. Resist the urge to push your shoulder down. The actual position of the shoulder is important, but it is more important that your nervous system feels safe doing it. This will make it more likely to engage the stabilizing muscles later when doing the same movement.

When you find an area of the body that feels like it is working too hard, this can easily cause pain and is also an indication that the sympathetic fight-or-flight system is firing. Slow this movement down enough that you can find the moment you begin to feel the increase in effort, the guarding or activation. What do you notice about that moment? Does it feel weak? Does it feel restricted? Does it feel scary or vulnerable? Is there some emotion associated with that movement? Once you have heard your body speak about that moment, then you can invite healing. If it is tight, you can mindfully stretch the area. If it is weak, mindfully strengthen that area. If there is an emotional component to that posture, attend to that emotion, getting professional mental health help if needed. If feeling that emotion does not push you out of your window of tolerance, if you can stay connected to your body as you feel the emotion, go ahead and feel it. Express it either verbally or through body movement, while ensuring that you stay connected to your body, as your indicator that you are staying within your window of tolerance.

Building Safety and Resilience Through Nutrition

WE ALL KNOW ABOUT OUR big brain, the one that thinks, makes decisions, and stores our memories. However, we also have a little brain. That little brain is our gut, which includes the stomach and the small and large intestine. Our gut contains a massive amount of nerve endings constantly responding to a variety of environmental stimuli. Our gut registers the foods we eat and manages how we break each food down into usable materials. Our gut regulates how much water and nutrients our body needs to keep, or be removed. Our gut is incredibly amazing.

Not only does the gut regulate all things related to our nourishment, but it also responds to our emotions and helps in regulating hormones such as stress hormones. Our little brain is in constant communication with our big brain about our state of wellness. This communication is called the gut-brain axis. Research has discovered that the communication between the gut and the brain is intricate and largely dependent on the gut biome. The gut biome, or microbiome, is the internal environment within our gut, including the community of micro-organisms that live in balance to maintain good physical and emotional health.

These microorganisms are affected by our diet, medication, and lifestyle. We are still in the early stages of understanding the significance of the gut biome, but we know that having a flourishing gut biome, resulting in a balanced nervous system, requires eating prebiotic and probiotic foods. Prebiotic foods support and nourish the gut biome, while probiotic foods replenish organisms in the gut. Probiotic foods include fermented foods and yogurt with active cultures. Building a gut biome is important when your gut has been drastically altered by things like a colonoscopy prep, antibiotics, or illness.

What we put into our little brain affects how it functions. So, our nutrition matters. There are an unlimited number of diet suggestions for good health. I will not address any of them specifically, as our nutrition needs differ based on our lifestyle, genetics, and ethical convictions. Let's look at some common threads in nutrition that affect our nervous system health and safety. These common threads include inflammation, chemicals, supplements or medications, sodium, and stimulants.

Inflammatory Foods

Inflammation is a sign that our body is in a state of stress, in other words, sympathetic activation. Inflammation can be local in one place in the body, such as after an injury. But inflammation can exist in the whole of the body, creating pain and disease. Our nutrition, movement, and stress levels affect inflammation levels in our whole body, causing us to be in a more sympathetic activated state. If you have chronic pain, you have inflammation, and nutrition is one of the tangible ways to address inflammation.

The link between our nutrition and our nervous system goes both ways. When we are in an activated sympathetic (fight-or-flight) state, we are more likely to trigger an inflammatory response with food allergies or sensitivities. Avoiding foods that create an inflammatory response will give our body a chance to find a deeper level of calm, or ventral vagal safety. However, hypervigilance with avoiding certain foods may strengthen a sympathetic fight-or-flight response, preventing us from reaching the ventral vagal state. The ideal goal would be to avoid inflammatory foods as a gift to your body, rather than a rule to be obeyed.

Some foods are universally inflammatory such as sugar, and others are universally anti-inflammatory. Turmeric/curcumin is an anti-inflammatory dietary supplement/spice that can be used to decrease inflammation. An anti-inflammatory diet can be used to calm the system after an inflammatory or activated season of life, to give the gut and the nervous system a rest while we do other exercises to encourage ventral vagal safety. We can use our gut to give our nervous system a leg up, to increase the probability of success.

Sugars

The effect of sugars on our system is significant. Our body needs sugar for energy, but excess sugars cause inflammation, addiction, and a host of other negative effects. Cancer cells love sugar as do many viruses. Too much sugar can cause pain and disease, or even death. It is no small thing. But not all sugars are created equal.

When talking about sugars, which can have a profoundly negative impact on our health, our goal is not to create danger in the foods we stay away from. A sense that some foods are dangerous may trigger our nervous system into a sympathetic activated state, which itself can cause the inflammation we are trying to decrease when avoiding sugars. So, we will take a balanced approach.

First, what is sugar? Sugar is obviously the white crystals we think of immediately. But it also includes brown sugars, coconut sugars, maple syrup, and honey among others. They are not created equal. Maple syrup and honey have not been heavily processed, which means they also have other trace nutrients that have benefits. But they are still sugar. This means that your body needs insulin to manage the sugar rush created when eating or drinking these sugars.

Glycemic index is a measure of how hard it is for your body to manage the sugar rush. A low glycemic index means that the sugar is broken down slowly, leading to a smaller sugar high and a smaller sugar crash, which is easier for our pancreas to keep up with the necessary insulin. A low glycemic sugar is the preferred sugar, especially in those with diabetes or pre-diabetes. Low glycemic diets are also preferred to encourage regulation of our nervous systems. Of the list of sugars above, coconut sugar is the lowest glycemic index, meaning that it is the better sugar for our pancreas, which secretes the insulin to manage sugar intake.

Carbohydrates are also sugars. These are more complex sugars, containing much needed fibre. Grains, fruit, and vegetables are carbohydrates that take more effort to break down into basic usable sugars. Generally, vegetables have a lower glycemic index compared to fruit.

Grains have been a point of contention. Wheat has been shown to increase gut permeability (leaky gut), causing inflammation and a variety of health problems (Perlmutter, 2018). This has led to a wave of people becoming gluten-free. However, many processed gluten-free substitutes primarily use rice flour, which has a very high glycemic index. As we avoid wheat and other gluten grains, we are gravitating to an equally unhealthy, but cheap to produce, rice flour which produces an unhealthy sugar high.

Chemical Foods

Avoiding foods with added chemicals such as preservatives and sprays is helpful for our nervous system because many of these chemicals directly affect our nervous system, or indirectly through our hormones or our gut biome.

Organic food is something that has been grown or raised without the use of chemicals. Some foods are typically more exposed to chemicals than others. These are known as the dirty dozen. Organic foods are typically more expensive because it is harder to grow food that looks pleasing enough to sell in a store while keeping the critters away. In addition to the dirty dozen, consider reading the list of foods that typically have less chemical exposure and are just as healthy to buy non-organic. Those lists are included in the list of additional resources at the end of the book.

While it would be great to be organic as much as possible, we can receive a significant improvement in our nervous system health simply by choosing foods that are less processed, closer to its original form. Some common hiding places of these chemicals might be prepared sauces, dips, and salad dressings. Food that comes in a can or frozen in a box is likely highly processed, containing higher amounts of chemical substances with a lower nutritional value.

Supplements and Medications

In an ideal world, we should be getting our nutrients from our food, but sometimes we can't do that. On the west coast where I live, it is very challenging to get enough vitamin D in the winter, when we hardly see the sun. So, supplementing when needed can be an appropriate response to our living conditions.

The view that supplements are always safe because they are natural is simply not true. If they have an effect, they have a side effect. There are many natural substances that are not safe to eat.

Supplements are like medications or food, there is an appropriate amount that we need. So, it is crucial to know the side effects and appropriate dosages of the supplements you are taking as well as your existing levels of the supplement you are adding.

Some supplements can directly help our nervous system find ventral vagal safety more easily. You can check with your medical professional if these are right for you.

Medications also have an effect and a side effect. In some circles, medications have been demonized. But some medications are completely necessary. The medications we take may have effects that either activate or dampen our nervous system. But we may need the primary effect of the medication to stay alive. If this is the case, it might be more challenging to achieve nervous system regulation while taking these medications. In those cases, you may need to be even more diligent in other areas of your life to help you reach ventral vagal safety.

Caffeine and Stimulants

Caffeine, sugars, and other stimulants will activate our nervous system. When our nervous system has a history of associating danger with activation, stimulants can draw our nervous system into a sympathetic fight-or-flight state. This can make it more difficult to bring our nervous system back to a ventral vagal safe state.

Caffeine is also a diarrhetic, which can negatively impact our hydration. This is further explained in the hydration section.

Generalities

The best diet for your nervous system is one that does not shame you into a dorsal vagal shutdown state or create a list of dangerous foods that bring you into sympathetic danger response. The best diet is one that is aware of the foods and eating patterns that promote health and well-being and being attracted to those.

Also, the best diet includes deciding to stay away from or limiting the intake of foods that make it more difficult to be in the ventral vagal safety state, especially during seasons of higher stress when your nervous system is already nearing its limit.

The Food We Eat

As we've just seen, the foods we eat affect our nervous system. How we eat our food also affects our nervous system. This section will not suggest a diet to follow for a healthy nervous system because there are many eating suggestions out there, some better than others, and none are right for everyone. So, we will talk about principles of eating with the goal of having more safety and resilience in our nervous system.

Many of us have built an unhealthy relationship with food. This might be related to societal pressures, learned behaviour from others with unhealthy patterns, or media messaging. It may also be physiological as the industrial age created a huge industry of processed foods with addictive qualities such as sodium and sugars. The added chemicals in our food are activating pleasure centres in the brain, making it difficult to stop. At the same time, society heaps unrealistic expectations on physique, which puts us at odds with the food that is meant to nourish us.

These societal conditions prepare us to be in a sympathetic activation state in relation to our food. Food is now the enemy that we must conquer or a form of trickery, promising us ventral safety but not delivering it.

The ventral vagal safety state is sometimes referred to as *rest and digest*. It is only when we feel safe that we divert our energy to effective digestion. When there is a threat, our body is reserving energy for the survival response of fight-or-flight. It does this by diverting energy away from the gut.

Medical conditions may arise when this energy is chronically diverted. With consistently less energy for digestion we may develop ulcers, irritable bowel disease, dyspepsia, heartburn, and Crohn's disease. All these conditions are strongly associated with a dysregulated nervous system caused by stress and/or trauma. Learning to regulate our nervous system to root us in a ventral vagal state can help heal these gut disorders.

Stress Eating

During my burnout a couple decades ago, I learned that my stress response was eating Cheezies. If you are from outside Canada, you may not know about these crunchy cheesy bits of salty goodness. Decades ago, completely depleted of energy, I ate Cheezies for dinner, a few times. I was horrified, of course, but this was my only available comfort at the time. Knowing what I know now, my nervous system was trying desperately to get to a rest and digest state. What I learned is that stress eating is self-defeating. Our bodies, desperately trying to push itself to rest and digest adds more food to digest, seemingly hoping that this increase in digestive demand pushes us into the ventral vagal state. Of course, it does not, often because the foods we eat at that time are also stimulating our nervous system, while we are needing it to calm itself. As a case in point, when I tried Cheezies when not stressed, I was surprised at how unappealing they were. As I connected to my nervous system during this experiment, I realized that the intense saltiness actually pushed my nervous system into the overwhelmed and disconnected dorsal vagal state, which felt like a relief when I was feeling the effects of stress, but was not healthy in so many ways. So, when I was in high stress, it provided the release valve to push me to dorsal vagal, and not feel the effects of sympathetic activation involved in stress. A more healthful eating pattern when under stress would be foods that increase safe reconnection with self. True comfort foods will not dull our senses, but will ignite a deeper compassionate connection to ourselves.

When we are under stress, especially threat, we lose the ability to make good decisions because our frontal cortex goes offline. We must, therefore, learn the road signs that tell us that we are not doing well in our inner being, or in our nervous system. For me, one of those road signs is Cheezies. The moment I have a craving for them, I must do a self check because there is a good chance that all is not well in my inner being. They are my proverbial canary in a mineshaft to tell me that there is something I need to attend to.

When we are in a state of stress, we are not well-connected to our bodies. When this happens, we will not be eating what our bodies need because we have no way of hearing what it needs. We won't hear our body tell us that it is hungry or thirsty. We won't feel the craving for vegetables or protein that our bodies give us when we are connected to it. So, we may miss meals, pushing our bodies into a stress response because it thinks it might starve. Or we may eat constantly because we are not connected enough to our bodies to hear the message of satiation when our bellies are full. Or we may be eating completely the wrong thing, when we are legitimately hungry, needing nourishment, but we fill our bellies with things of little nutritional value.

Elimination Tips

What goes in must come out. So, let's talk elimination in the context of our nervous system. We want to learn the rhythms of our bodies and then notice when they fall out of rhythm. When our bodies change their rhythm, we should be asking ourselves why. There may be a very normal reason why things change, such as with a diet rich in beets. But changes in elimination may also tell you about the state of our nervous system.

If we have settled into a sympathetic or dorsal vagal state, noticing our elimination habits might be triggering. Learning the ideal frequency of a bowel movement might heap pressure on us, bringing us more into a sympathetic state, and thus, further unable to have regular bowel movements. Obviously, this is not helpful. Rather than evaluating with a sense of goodness or badness about bowel movements, consider bowel movements as another way to communicate with your nervous system, to notice if it is in ventral vagal or not. We don't fix the nervous system through our elimination. We learn about our nervous system through elimination. What comes out of our little brains (gut) is an indication of what is happening inside the little, and big, brain. It is not the source of the problem itself.

Adequate bowel movements are ideally at least once a day, first thing in the morning. Bowel movements should be easy and well-formed. When we are not well hydrated or if we lack enough fibre, it will not be easy and well-formed. This can be a message to adjust our eating and drinking patterns.

Pushing a bowel movement is not a great idea. In the Western world, our toilet heights have not done us any favours. The mechanics of our pelvic floor is built to eliminate best in a squat position. That means that we may be working too hard to eliminate if our knees are not higher than our hips. Using a stool in our bathroom can help raise the knees, allowing us to stay relaxed for a more efficient elimination. Yes, I said it, use a stool for your stool.

The rhythm of a morning bowel movement is the result of a nervous system that has successfully gone into a rest and digest state (i.e., ventral vagal) at night when we are designed to do just that. A glass of water in the morning can help stimulate the gut to produce that morning bowel movement. But you may also need to look at your morning routine to make sure that you have given yourself the time and space to ensure that your gut is happy and on board for the day. Mornings with elements of calm and safety will help your gut feel relaxed enough to empty. It may be helpful to review the tips in the sleeping section for comments on transitioning your nervous system from sleep to wakefulness.

Nutrition Exercises for Nervous System Safety and Resilience

➤ **First steps:** Learning about the connection between the foods we eat, how and when we eat may have given you a long list of things you want to change. Rather than overwhelming yourself trying to conquer this list, consider one thing to add to your dietary routine, a food, or a practice, and one thing to take away or limit that will help heal your gut.

Remember that we want to be kind to our nervous system, so please resist the temptation to go extreme. The goal here is to create a gut environment of healing. That will set you up for better hormone regulation, including stress hormones, as well as better nutrient uptake. Having a more peaceful gut will help the nervous system find safety and rest, allowing even greater healing in other areas of life.

When you are eating, start to notice the level of stress or anxiety you are feeling. Now, try slowing down your chewing speed. Do you notice how your nervous system calms? To increase safety in your nervous system, slow down your eating. Slow down the chewing of food, the cutting of food and slowing down how quickly it comes to your mouth.

➤ **Next steps:** Create a friendly, non-shaming reminder around places you go to for food, to remind yourself to check in to your body. Tie a bow around the fridge handle, or put a happy face sticker on the snack drawer handle, or sticky note in your lunch box asking you how you are.

These can be your reminders to bring you back to connection to your body as you eat. It is important that these are viewed as your body inviting you back into connection rather than a shaming thing to do. We do not want to push you into a shutdown state where it is even more difficult to reconnect with self. This should be a kind invitation.

What do you notice as you eat with awareness, in connection with your body? Are there messages of hunger or satiation that you were surprised by? Did you notice any progression of road signs along the way to hunger or satiation? Did "hungry" and "full" come up suddenly? If it did, bring your awareness to the sensation of hungry and full and see if you can work backwards a little to notice a sensation that might have clued you in to the fact that you were getting close to hungry or close to full. This exercise is not meant to make you more hypervigilant to these sensations, but rather to teach you more words in the language of your nervous system, in how your body communicates to you regarding your nutrition.

Advanced steps: As you eat today, bring your awareness to your inner self. Do you view some foods as dangerous? Notice what that physically feels like inside when you contemplate eating that "dangerous" food. I'm not talking about things that are actually dangerous to eat such as poison. I'm referring to foods that you may have demonized in your good intentions to gain better gut health. This might be a specific food, or additive or a food group. As you notice the sensation of danger in some foods, do you notice the same sensation come up with other unexpected foods that don't have any negative nutritional effect? In other words, did your avoidance of unhealthful foods leak into other areas, affecting your relationship with neutral or healthful foods?

Notice how your nervous system responds as you eat different foods. Be careful that you don't give your sympathetic nervous system full rein to find enemies and threats everywhere. We want a compassionate look at our bodies and how they respond to foods. Notice which foods make you feel good inside. Not the immediate sugar-rush good feeling that happens in the same part of the brain that is activated with any other addiction. Notice which foods or eating habits make you more inclined to live your best life or make you feel a little more empowered. Notice if there is a correlation between your food and your desire to be physically active. What foods make you want to get outside and enjoy people and nature versus foods that make you want to zone out.

Can you identify the physical sensation of the sugar rush? This addictive activation can happen with other foods, usually with additives to heighten taste, and can drive eating past what you need for good nutrition. Consider using this sensation as your yield sign. To stop eating for a moment, reconnect with your body, and then decide if you want to continue to eat so you don't defer that decision to the addictive centre of your brain.

Hydration

Humans are on average about 60 percent water. This means that we need to hydrate our bodies to create a safe and happy self. Our nervous systems will more easily be in the safety of ventral vagal if it is not struggling to perform basic functions, which require water. If we are dehydrated, our bodies will register that there is a threat to survival. When there is a survival threat, we will not be in a ventral vagal state. Therefore, we must view hydration as an important piece of physical and emotional health.

Hydration directly affects our nervous system because fluids are the mechanism to get survival nutrients to every system including the nervous system. When we are dehydrated, we can experience the odd flutter of our heart, which is controlled by our nervous system. This flutter is an expression of a sympathetic activation. This is evidence of how dehydration can cause an increase in sympathetic activation, making it more difficult to return to ventral vagal calm.

Technically, physical signs of dehydration include fatigue, feeling of thirst, headache, confusion, and changes in urine. However, dehydration occurs much earlier than that. Fatigue for example: if you are slouched, unable to do anything, you might be dehydrated. Also, if you are unmotivated, or a bit lazy, this can be an earlier version of fatigue caused by dehydration. A headache might be caused by dehydration, but an earlier version of the dehydration headache might be a sluggish brain. Especially in a typical high-sodium North American diet, we are likely dehydrated a lot more often than we think and it affects our health in significant ways.

How to Hydrate

The long-time gold standard for hydration is eight glasses of water a day. There is a huge variation in the necessary water consumption in a day but, aiming for about eight glasses for an average adult in average temperatures doing mild to moderate activity would be a good rough goal to start. The key is to be aware of your water intake and how you feel when you are well hydrated. This will take some time to figure out for you and your activity level.

The amount of water a person needs varies. On hot days, we will need more than the base amount of water. On days of heavy sweating with exercise or manual labour jobs, you will need more water. When the humidity in the air is less, we will need to drink more water because we are losing more moisture to the air.

How we take in the water also matters. Much like the forgotten plant wilting in the crusty soil, if we dump a lot of water on the dry plant, the soil can't take it in. We don't want to stress the kidneys with a large intake of water all at once. It is not absorbed well, and it is hard on the kidneys. Even if we find ourselves quite dehydrated, sipping water is much more effective than gulping glasses at a time.

The temperature of your water also matters. Because the path from the esophagus to the stomach is wrapped in vagus nerve fibres, any shock to the system can cause some irritation of the vagus nerve. Warm water can help ease a stomach in tension much like a heating pad can ease muscle pain. Switching our water from ice water to room temperature or hot water can be enough to encourage the stomach to relax, making it easier to be in the ventral vagal safety state.

Coffee does not count for water intake because any caffeine that we eat or drink will dehydrate us. It takes an additional one to two cups of water for each cup of coffee just to break even. Staying or becoming hydrated may require a decrease in caffeine intake levels.

Some medications also cause dehydration. This might alter how much water you should be drinking in a day. Please discuss this with your doctor.

Sodium

Most processed foods are high in sodium and other chemicals that can cause dehydration. While some sodium is needed for nerve function, a typical North American diet is too high in sodium. This excess sodium causes water to be drawn to where it is not needed, causing stress on our kidneys, our lymphatic system, and affecting blood pressure making the heart work harder. This increase in stress on our organs prevents our nervous system from reaching a ventral vagal state because the baseline activation of our heart will be higher. A simple way to make it easier to find safety and resilience is to decrease our sodium intake.

Elimination

An awareness of our urination patterns can tell us about our hydration and our nervous system in the same way bowel elimination does.

Urination should occur every two and a half to four hours with an output of about twelve to twenty-five seconds of uninterrupted flow to empty. Urine should be light yellow in colour with only a mild odour. Women typically have a smaller bladder than men on average. If your urine is normally a strong yellow colour, you are likely dehydrated and/or you are overdosing, and eliminating excess supplements such as vitamin B.

A person with a regulated nervous system will be able to easily transition between holding their bladder closed and emptying their bladder. If we are waiting awhile on the toilet before our bladder empties, our nervous system doesn't yet have the resilience to easily transition to the relaxed state needed to urinate. If this is the case, resist the temptation to push the urine out. Because of the mechanics of the bladder, this is counterproductive and can cause problems. If you have a sensation that your bladder doesn't fully empty, it could be because your nervous system is not getting to ventral vagal relaxation, which is required to eliminate fully. This is called a *nervous bladder*. Let's remember that we don't fix the nervous system by forcing the bladder to comply with fully emptying. We build safety and resilience in our nervous system in as many ways as possible, so our bladder willingly empties as it was designed to do.

Hydration Exercises for Nervous System Safety and Resilience

➤ **First steps:** Start your day with a glass of water, sipped over the span of about an hour. Gradually reduce your caffeine intake, if needed, to encourage a more peaceful nervous system and a water intake target you can achieve. Start to notice how it feels before and after drinking water, and appreciate the sensation of being better hydrated.

➤ **Next steps:** Create some habits that encourage hydration through your day. Think of your home environment, work environment, any place that you spend significant time. Start some habits to increase your awareness of the need for water. Try to think through your habit-making plan in a way that is attainable. You don't want lofty goals with numbers that you will fail at and then chastise yourself when you don't meet the goals. When you chastise yourself like this, the result is most often that you will push yourself into either sympathetic activation (i.e., anger) or dorsal vagal shutdown (i.e., shame). You don't want to do that. You want to create a healthful lifestyle. Start with finding one lifestyle shift you can make to increase your hydration. Once that shift has become a habit, you can add another. This will increase the likelihood of not jumping into the competitive-style goal-setting that does not help your nervous system find safety.

As you go about your day, try to increase your awareness of your thirst response. When you feel thirsty, take a moment before you quench the thirst to notice what thirst feels like. Once you have identified what thirst feels like to your body, see if you can notice a less intense version of the same sensation. Most of us don't notice the message to drink until we are quite dehydrated. The goal here is to start to notice when your body is needing water before it is desperate for it. Then, when you quench your thirst, feel the sensation of a quenched thirst, and savour it.

As you increase your awareness of your sensation of thirst, do you need to adjust your target hydration for the day to stay fully hydrated? Often what we thought of as hydration wasn't quite as well hydrated as we thought. Start noticing the shifts of your hydration needs based on activities or environmental conditions.

Advanced steps: Now that you have some habits to stay hydrated, try to notice how your nervous system feels when you are hydrated or dehydrated. When you are dehydrated, do you notice that you are a little more on edge or irritable? Do you notice a little more tension in your body compared to when you are fully hydrated? Do you feel how your tissues feel a little more supple and willing to move when you are hydrated? Try to notice and feel these sensations, bringing these responses to your awareness.

Notice how your hydration messages change with your mood. Do you have a craving for water when you get nervous or anxious or waiting with anticipation? When we are in a sympathetic state, our system requires more water because our metabolism goes up, as we prepare to fight or flee, which often results in sweating. This response can explain the dry mouth feeling when we are anxious.

If you go the whole day hardly drinking water and not feeling a sense of thirst, it could be that you are not as connected to yourself as you could be. If that is the case, go back and do some of the first step exercises from the body and movement chapter to establish better communication with your body and try it again. There is no human alive who doesn't need water.

Building Safety and Resilience with Your Life

SO FAR WE HAVE SEEN how our physical body, both the structure and nutrition of it, affects our nervous system. We have explored ways to use that connection to build safety and resilience in our nervous system. Now we will explore the connection of our nervous system to how we live.

We will now look at a few aspects of life and how they relate to our nervous system. By understanding how they relate, we can make some adjustments or nudge our comfort in certain areas to help our overall nervous system health, leading to greater safety and resilience.

Our lives are full of interactions that can help stabilize our nervous systems, or cause us to go into dysregulation. We can become dysregulated by surrounding ourselves with the chaos of last-minute holiday shopping, but a caring friend can help us regulate back to a state of calm. These ups and downs can include how we relate to other people, how we have fun, and how we connect to our deeper self. Rather than avoiding people, fun, or our deeper self, we can use these challenges as exercises to build a stronger nervous system.

Connecting to self and others is key to good vagal function. Remember that the vagus nerve connects to structures of the face and neck as well as body organs. The vagus nerve is connected to what Stephen Porges calls the *social engagement system*. This is the big nerve network that makes human connections (i.e., relationships) possible. This includes our ability to read social cues and facial expressions. This is the system that activates the warm fuzzies when we get a hug from a dear friend or when we have meaningful eye contact with another living thing. This is the system that makes authentic, meaningful connection with others possible.

If you have recently spent a significant amount of time in a dorsal vagal state, the description I gave of the social engagement system might seem terrifying. Don't panic. Once you've spent some time with the body and nutrition exercises in the previous chapters, the exercises here will be easier. Remember your guardrails and anchors. If you get the sensations of activation or shutdown, pause the exercise, go back to a safety anchor, and when things stabilize, try again. Some activation is expected as we do the exercises. As long as you can stay present with your body in the activated state, you may continue with the exercise.

This section includes components of life that are not directly body related. But they are aspects of life that have a strong vagal component. This means that we can use them to learn about our nervous system and to help expand our window of tolerance as we build a stronger nervous system.

Sleep

The power of a good sleep is undeniable. Maybe you can remember a great sleep when you woke up feeling rested and ready for the day. For many people with pain or nervous system dysregulation, these days do not happen often.

Sleep is the healing time for our body. The ventral vagal safety state is often described as the rest and digest state. During this time of sleep, our body is busy absorbing the nutrients we need from the food we eat. For that reason, effective sleep can improve digestive problems. Because we are not expending energy moving our physical body while sleeping, this is a time of restoration and healing from the activities of the previous day.

During an active day, our postural muscles and our moving muscles are in various states of contraction. That contraction doesn't allow the dissipation of any accumulating inflammation to happen. When we sleep, those muscles can relax, allowing inflammation and the naturally occurring debris from the work of movement to dissipate. This is especially true for brain health. A good sleep will allow the brain to clean up debris that is thought to lead to plagues such as dementia or even multiple sclerosis. One of the first goals of any healing program should include restoration of sleep. Once you are sleeping in a relaxed state, in unity with the circadian rhythms, healing in all other areas will be much easier.

I'm sure we have all had those days where we were racing to finish a task before bed. Our heart rate might be increased, our gut a little tight with the anxiety of trying to finish our tasks. We finally finish, declaring to ourselves that it is now time for bed. We go to bed, exhausted, our body easily tired but we sleep in fits and starts, if we sleep at all. We wake up often in the night or have frantic dreams. This does not feel like a restful sleep. What went wrong?

Let's think back to principles of putting a baby to sleep. We know it is nearly bedtime, so we start to quiet the house, perhaps turn on some relaxing, lilting music. We speak more softly to the baby, and we slow our actions and our speech. Maybe we give the baby a warm bath and snuggle them in a fuzzy blanket. The lights are dimmed as you feed the baby one last time. We have been deliberate about a nighttime routine to get baby to sleep, and none of that routine includes frantic activity, loud voices, or bright lights. We have prepared the baby's nervous system to enter a ventral vagal rest and digest state to help bring about a deeper sleep.

The good news is that these principles also work for the rest of us. Regardless of how grown you are, teen or adult, we have more responsibility than an infant. It is, therefore, more difficult to let those responsibilities go for hours at a time while we sleep. Rather than assuming that we are doomed to a life of poor sleep, we can do things to help strengthen our ventral vagal system and invite it to greater influence in our sleep life.

Any of the other exercises in this book will help increase the capacity of your ventral vagal system and may automatically result in improvements in sleep. The ability to get to sleep and stay asleep is a reflection of the resilience of your nervous system to shift from activation that is needed during the day to a surrendered calm required for sleep.

The more we fret about our sleep, the worse it will become because the fretting activates the nervous system. It is like a volume dial that needs to be dialled all the way to zero before sleep. If we activate all the way to the max all day long, it will take longer and much more "effort" to bring the dial back to zero. The goal is to activate appropriately during the day and to increase the responsivity of the dial so it has a better chance of getting to zero when it is time to sleep.

Preparing Your Nervous System for Sleep

Having a sleep routine is important for the circadian rhythms within our body. There is a mountain of research to support this and if this is an area of interest, consider looking at a more detailed source of information. I will stay general, so as to not overwhelm and bury you with details.

Our circadian rhythm is meant to align with daylight. You may have heard of the health challenges for those who work night shifts. This is because their circadian rhythms do not match with the rising and setting of the sun.

If you are someone who predominantly sleeps while the sun is up but want healing in your life, be prepared for changes to occur. Shifting your sleep-wake cycle to match daylight more closely can be a challenge. But it can be done. Shifting your sleep schedule is much more easily initiated with your waking schedule compared to your sleeping schedule. Deciding that you will get to bed earlier rarely works. Forcing yourself to get up a little earlier is much more possible, and this can make you more ready to sleep a little earlier. When you start shifting your rhythm you might be sleepy during the day as your previous habits object to the new patterns. Change takes time and it is not comfortable. But, sleeping roughly when the sun is down will allow for a better sleep, better healing, and better digestion.

Preparing Your Nervous System for Wakefulness

Living an embodied life starts in the first moments of wakefulness. Being embodied means that we live our lives with an awareness of and presence within our physical body. This doesn't mean that our conscious brain constantly analyzes our body sensations. In fact, those who live a life in perpetual hypervigilance of every bodily sensation are in a fear relationship with their body, which does not promote healing. In an embodied approach to health, we want to be present in and at peace with our bodies, willing to hear messages the body tells us but not frantically looking for signs of danger.

The first moments of the day can set the tone for the activities of the day. When we were sleeping, we were at the deepest form of rest we were able to attain. In those moments, we perceive the least threats, and this is the safest time of our day. If we feel desperate to hold on to the safety of the bed, we jump out of bed without connecting to our bodies. It can be as if we've left our nervous system in bed where it is safe. It would be much better if we gratefully said goodbye to our safe haven of rest and invited our body and nervous system to be present with us during our day.

To do that, you can start your day with a gradual increase in activation to connect to your body. A body scan would work and can be very quick as you simply take stock of how your body is doing today. Start with moving a couple body parts, hands or feet. You may notice that there is tension somewhere in your body. If you can, do a little stretch of that tightness while still in bed. You are not looking for problems, but you are resourcing your body to help it carry you through your day. You can then mentally assess your mind and spirit, asking what you might need to thrive through the day. You may tell yourself an affirmation or literally give yourself a pat on the back. You could do a mindfulness meditation or if you are a spiritual person, you could pray, chant, or resource your inner self and its relationship with the divine to embrace whole person health and safety. Ensure that you are connecting to yourself as you are deciding what you need that day.

Practical Tips to Encourage Neurological Safety in Sleep

The space you sleep in can either promote safety or threat in your nervous system. While we often deliberately choose colours or patterns that are softer in a bedroom, we also need to view the space with a greater sense of safety. Thinking about the things that are activating for you, are there any reminders of those in the space you do your nighttime routine? Are there any work reminders or electronics nearby? Consider moving them to a different space in your home to help encourage your nervous system to only feel safety before bed. This is the same for pictures of people who've been unloving toward you.

Watching television or having a device in bed does not give your nervous system a clear message that it is time to sleep. This can give conflicting messages to your nervous system resulting in ineffective sleep preparation. Consider moving your entertainment to a place other than the place you sleep.

Electronics and Wi-Fi can activate people's nervous systems. Consider wired internet instead of Wi-Fi, or turn the modem itself completely off at night when it is time to sleep. The same should be done with cell phones. Keeping an active cell phone by your bed can be enough activation for some people to prevent a reliably restorative sleep from happening.

Blue light from screens and electronics mimics sunshine and stimulates the brain to a sense of waking up. Exposure to blue light in the last six hours of our wakeful day will confuse your system. It tells us that it is morning, urging us to wake up, which is the opposite of the message we want to convey at that time. The goal with creating sleep hygiene is to develop clear messages to our nervous system about its role, to either wake us up or prepare for sleep and digestion.

Sleeping Positions

Stomach sleeping is the only position widely discouraged among medical practitioners and yet, is still a common preferred sleeping position. Generally, rationale based on body mechanics is used to support this argument. And these mechanical challenges are significant. Stomach sleepers must maintain neck rotation to breathe. This can cause persistent neck pain or headaches, as well as be a source of a fascial pull that causes a twist in other areas of our body. Not only could we have physical pain because of stomach sleeping, associated compression through the upper neck can irritate the vagus nerve. This mechanical irritation of the vagus nerve may negatively affect its function and may contribute to poor nervous system resilience.

Stomach sleepers tend to have an intense desire to be in that position. What is it about that position that brings us so much peace? Being a recovering stomach sleeper myself, I noticed that I have a desire to spend at least a few minutes on my stomach on days that have been more emotionally stressful. It turns out, this makes sense with nervous system anatomy.

When we live our life in a highly activated state, we may find it difficult to settle our nervous system to allow sleep to happen. Pressure on the front of the chest and abdomen can help the ventral vagal system activate its brake on the sympathetic nervous system. This was recently investigated with the use of weighted blankets to help calm children with autism. It turns out, this works with most people.

If you are presently in an activated state, try this now. If not, wait until you are in a slightly activated state. Tune in to your level of activation and place one hand over your breastbone and one over the top part of the abdomen, just below your ribs. Your hands should have a gentle, flat contact. Add gradually more pressure to each of your hands and note the level of activation. In most cases, you will notice your level of activation drop as you feel your muscles relax, your breath deepening, and you may feel a sense of physical heaviness as your body sinks into relaxation.

If you are a stomach sleeper, it is important to understand what draws you to that position. For the health of your neck, it would be best to teach your body to sleep in another position. But that transition will be more successful by improving the health of your nervous system or simply doing the pressure exercise described above.

For your nervous system, sleeping on your back is a position of complete surrender to sleep if the legs and arms are in a relaxed position. However, back sleeping has a higher correlation with sleep apnea. Sleep apnea is a condition when you stop the regular breathing patterns and often results in gasping for air. This can be due to gravity on the structures of the throat and nasal passages. The lack of oxygen and the gasping for air forces the nervous system into a state of sympathetic arousal as it feels a sense of survival urgency, even if just for a moment. As a result, people with sleep apnea do not feel rested, they do not get as much time in the restorative sleep stages and are not as well oxygenated. Also, their nervous systems do not reach ventral vagal rest, and are more likely to have sympathetic activation such as anxiety or digestive disorders.

Side sleeping avoids the challenges of stomach or back sleeping, and it is generally the most widely recommended sleeping position. Incidentally, this is also the closest position to the one we were in when we were safely tucked in a uterus, getting ready to enter the unpredictable and sometimes dangerous world. Perhaps our nervous systems remember this position as one of safety.

Sleep Exercises for Nervous System Safety and Resilience

- **First steps:** Start with going outdoors at either sunrise or sunset, whichever is already available to you. The sun rays at that time communicate to your nervous system that it is either time to wake up at sunrise or time to prepare for sleep at sunset. Take in the sights. Notice how the sun hits your environment. Once you have done this, try to respect the messages of the universe to either start your day or end your day and choose activities accordingly. If you just watched the sunrise, do not climb into your pjs and into bed. Instead, do something as you would during your active day. If you just watched a sunset, do not start a new task, or turn on a bright light. Start thinking of what you need to finish to get some completion for the day. Do not have sugar or caffeine to activate your nervous system. This is a time to do quiet peaceful things, not tasks that activate or frustrate you. Start to align your activities to match the sun.

Next steps: Plan a nighttime routine that will bring you gradually from your normal speed of activity in the day to a place of rest. Think about the tasks you need to ready yourself for sleep and try to find a way to keep the more energetic tasks at the start of your routine and the more soothing tasks later when you need to be slower. For example, if you apply lotion, be deliberate about slow, relaxing movements rather than a focus on getting it done as quickly as possible. Attempt to slow the process down a little more than feels natural to you. Remember that you are trying to teach your nervous system a new way of being and a greater capacity to deliberately wind down.

Once in bed, tune in to your nervous system and observe your breath and your heart rate. Use the slow exhale breath described in the breathing section to encourage the parasympathetic relaxation. Deliberately slow the chatter in your brain...to...speak...very...slowly...to...yourself. If you read the previous statement slowly, as written, you have likely sighed by now, as your nervous system briefly slowed down. As you slow the chatter, notice how your body sinks into a deeper state of rest. Notice your breath become slower and deeper. If you are struggling to settle, add some soft pressure to your breastbone and upper abdomen, just below the ribs. As you do this, you should notice your muscles soften and relaxation deepen.

➤ **Advanced steps:** In an ideal world, our activity level will match our internal wake/sleep schedule. It is important to know what the transitions between the states feel like and then respect those transitions. Once you know what it feels like to have your nervous system gently wind down, let that take precedence. Listen to your body's message of sleep. Become more tuned in during those moments of early wakefulness and approaching sleep. When you are in bed, in those first moments of wakefulness, before you start moving, what does that moment feel like? Do you notice the degrees of wakefulness? Can you stay in that moment when your brain is awake, but it is not quite fully awake? Can you stay with it in compassionate observation to wait for your body to guide how quickly it wants to rouse from sleep and become fully awake? Do you then sense that moment when your body has an anticipation of movement? These are all the steps our body and nervous system take to wake us up in the morning. You can do the same in the evening. As you start to feel tired, notice what this physically feels like. What did pre-tired feel like? Try to notice and describe the sensations that led up to a feeling of being tired.

Increasing our awareness of our body's wakefulness process allows us to be more embodied during the day. In essence, we have not left our nervous system in the safety of the bed as we jump up to accomplish the first task of the day. We can respect the timing of our nervous system to allow it to fully transition from rest to activation without the threat of having been bullied into rapid chaotic morning energy.

Social Connection

Connecting with yourself and others can be a beautiful experience or a stressful one. The stress of connecting with others is particularly strong when we have been in a stressed or overwhelmed state. In those states, connection with others can feel like a double-edged sword. We crave the comfort and solace of others, but we have the urge to run away from people. Our nervous system does not have the capacity to do the thing that will help support us: to be with our trusted core people.

When our nervous system is in the safe state, social connections with others are relatively easy, even as an introvert. This can range from a superficial conversation about the weather with the person at the grocery checkout to deep conversation about our vision and passion in life with a trusted friend. Ventral vagal states allow social connection that is authentic and empathic. When we feel safe, we will find solace with eye contact from a caring person. We will feel the freedom and joy of huge laughter. And we will feel empathy toward others, near and far. In a ventral vagal state, we are connected to our trusted core, and anchored there. And we can also extend our compassion to others on the planet.

Our response to watching news stories can give us a good indication of how our nervous systems are. If we feel empathy toward those hurting by whatever catastrophe happened that day, then at least we know that our nervous system can connect to others, and thus, we are in a ventral vagal state. If watching the news causes us agitation, frustration, and cussing, we might be in a sympathetic activated state where we see danger rather than people. If we are in a dorsal overwhelm state, we may have chosen to not watch the news at all because it just feels like too much. If we are watching, we may feel defeated and helpless. How we see people and the world gives us a glimpse of our inner state of wellness.

In a sympathetic fight-or-flight state, our nervous system is in survival mode, which often means that conversation with others is oriented to the threats around us. We don't have to look further than the early days of the COVID-19 pandemic when everyone on the planet was going through their version of processing the threats of the unknown virus and all that entailed. Newsreels and chatter among friends, peers, and strangers were centred on what you or they were doing or not doing to manage the unknown. Talk about our deep passions or vision for our futures were not as frequent. When there is a perceived threat, we do not have time for deep connections.

The challenge in this situation is that any stress or trauma is best healed and recovered when witnessed and shared with someone. The easiest option would be to have a trusted being somehow know that we need connection and for them to initiate that connection. This can be a human, or a pet. Often, this intuitive connection does not happen. We can live busy and relatively isolated lives that make it difficult for others to know that we need connection. Think of the people who you are a trusted being for. Do you really know how each of those people are doing on a deep level on any given day or week? It is hard to stay connected to others enough to sense when they need us to reach out, and vice versa.

In an overwhelmed state, connection with others feels impossible. People might know that you are not well and reach out, but you may cancel plans with them because it is just too hard to be around people, even supportive and trusted people. Most of us have been in that state at least once in our lives. In your isolation, you are not alone. And there are things we can do to build our relational nervous system.

Connection Exercises for Nervous System Safety and Resilience

➤ **First steps:** If connecting with others is extremely difficult, start warming up your nervous system to the idea of connection by building resilience in the relationships that are already happening and where there is nothing to lose. The next time you are running errands, when the person at the checkout asks you some version of how you are doing or if you found everything you needed, *look up*! Look at their face when you respond to their question. You may feel your heart race a bit if you've been in overwhelm or depression for awhile, but remember, this person won't remember this interaction. You have nothing to lose. When that gets easy, try making eye contact. You can start with just a brief gaze and progress to holding eye contact for as long as it takes to answer their question. And then try adding a pleasant smile as you do this. You can fake it if you must. You are training your nervous system to connect with someone else's nervous system. It doesn't have to be a genuine smile. Even a fake smile will warm the other person to your connection, and you will be rewarded with an experience of a pleasant connection with another human being as they are likely to smile back.

➤ **Next steps:** As you go about your day, observe people's interactions, and consider what nervous system state they are in. Do you recognize people connecting in a safe ventral vagal way? What does that look like? Try to observe aspects of their interactions such as eye contact, posture, facial expressions, and physical touch. Do you recognize interactions where someone starts in fight-or-flight? Does the other person respond in the same fight-or-flight way? What if the other person was in ventral vagal safety? Does the fight-or-flight person activate the other, so both are now in fight-or-flight? Or does the ventral vagal safe person help bring safety to the fight-or-flight person? These are the dynamics of *co-regulation*. Our nervous system states respond to other nervous systems. This can encourage us to be more regulated or less. And co-regulation also means that we have the influence to help someone else regulate.

As you notice the differences in the connections around you, you are more likely to recognize when your nervous system is shifting while connecting with others. You will notice changes when you become defensive toward someone for no apparent reason, because you have entered fight-or-flight response, detecting a threat. In this case, the next step would be to determine if that person is truly a threat or triggering a threat. For example, maybe you didn't cognitively realize that you don't trust them, but your nervous system is detecting a threat. Maybe they remind you of someone who broke your trust, but they themselves haven't acted in an untrustworthy way. Understanding your responses in relationships will give you more information to guide you back to a sense of safety with your trusted core, and allow you to be open to the possibilities of welcoming others into your trusted core.

Advanced steps: Think back to some interactions you've had with people. These interactions could be easy, superficial, deep, meaningful, or even arguments. During these interactions, can you remember what your body felt like? Can you identify what nervous system state you were in at that moment by what you felt? Did it feel safe and connected (ventral vagal)? Did you feel nervous or threatened (sympathetic)? Or did you check out (dorsal vagal)? How might these interactions have been different if you were in a different state? For example, in the case of an argument or confrontation, how might that interaction have physically felt if you had been in a safe ventral state rather than a threatened sympathetic state? If we can look back at an interaction, even a hurtful one, and view it from a place of safety within ourselves, we may dissolve some of the emotional intensity of the interaction.

Boundaries

We can't talk about social connection without talking about boundaries. The goal with the previous exercises was to connect with trusted beings. But what if you are required to have some connection with people whom you do not trust? This is when we need boundaries.

When we talk about boundaries, we often think about learning to say no. While this is a necessity in life and is part of the action of setting boundaries, let's get a little more basic first so those "no" statements come from an authentic self. Let's look at nervous system boundaries.

Boundary Exercises for Nervous System Safety and Resilience

➤ **First steps:** Having boundaries requires that we first know ourselves. Wherever you are, start to feel the definition of your physical space by touching various parts of your body. This might seem very basic, and you will be tempted to skip this part. Please don't. As you physically touch the outer edge of your physical space, notice the sensation of your hand on the body part you are touching. This is the place that your body interacts with your world. Do you notice a difference in any place in your body? Do you notice places that don't want to be touched or places that crave touch? Do those differences determine how you interact with others? For example, if you don't like touch on your chest, do you cringe when someone comes in for a hug? Or, if you crave touch there, do you crave hugs and find security with a hug?

As you touch a body part with your hand, slowly release the touch and see if you can increase your awareness of the absolute minimum pressure needed to still feel touch. The goal here is to increase your awareness of the interface between your physical body and the outside world.

Next steps: We are not just physical bodies. We also have an electromagnetic field. Back in the day of the rabbit ear TV antennae, we were acutely aware that our electromagnetic field interacts with TV signals. It is this same energetic field that tells us when someone is "in our space." This electromagnetic field can change in depth and intensity. If we have a small field, we will allow people much closer to us before any alarm bells ring about their safety. It may also mean that your personal energy is on the smaller side, or it may mean that we've had a boundary violation there.

When we do this next exercise, we are not making any judgments about the goodness or badness of the depth of our energy field. We will be compassionate observers. As we observe the edges of our energetic field, the barrier we feel may change, just because it was observed.

Being aware of our energetic boundaries will help us decide who we bring in a little closer and who can stay energetically distant if they don't feel safe for us. The exercise itself might feel a little "woo-woo" but we are feeling a very real energetic field the same way you would feel a mild electrical current.

Starting with the palms of your hands facing your body, remind yourself of the limits of your physical body by touching it. Then, turn your palms facing outward, but still touching your body with the other side of your hand. Imagine you are slowly pushing your hands through water. As you slowly push your hands away from yourself, there will be a point where the water feels dense. Play with this edge a little and feel it. Back off from the edge and then come back on it. This is your energetic boundary of self.

Now, back off from the edge and slowly go out in a different direction to start to map out all your edges. This might look a little like the mime stuck in a box, but an irregular-shaped box, extending further from your body in some places and closer in other places.

Notice inside your body what it feels like to lightly push into that boundary, to feel the edge of your energetic space.

Advanced steps: As you practise feeling your energetic boundaries, you may have noticed a spot that your hand pushes straight through. If this is the case, you can go back to another spot nearby and feel that edge. Often when you do, the nearby spot with no boundary can start to spontaneously fill in, creating a boundary.

The theory behind the holes in the energetic boundary is that these physical places might be the entry point of a previous boundary violation. If the boundary doesn't spontaneously fill in or if, when you repeat the exercise, it comes up again and again, you may need to visit your trauma specialist or somatic counsellor to address the psychological aspects of that potential boundary violation.

In my experience, those places where there is an empty hole is also a place of vulnerability. When I have wondered why I said yes to something I didn't want to or failed to establish a boundary that needed to be placed, I consider where I was in the space relative to the person asking.

Sometimes, the person making the request is in a hole, where a boundary violation already occurred and hadn't yet been adequately resolved. Closing our energetic holes through this basic energetic exercise, supported by the guidance of a trauma professional if needed, will help us more consistently and confidently establish boundaries when we need to.

Play

Imagine a scene where a young child is playing with their energetic puppy. They take turns chasing each other around the room, embracing and running away, and returning to each other. They may be playing with a toy or rolling on the floor. You hear the giggles of the child and see the sloppy puppy kisses. Why does this scene bring us joy? Is this joy a message to our nervous system that is remembering the sweetness of safety, of feeling loved and accepted? Does this scene bring us joy as we remember the moments of being fully in the present, with no concern for what is happening around us or for what is ahead of us? This is the picture of ventral vagal safety.

At the time of writing, there is very little research done on adult playfulness. The scant research that exists supports the idea that those with a higher level of playfulness also have healthier relationships and are physically healthier.

Understanding the nervous systems states, this makes sense. When we picture play, we do not picture someone who is fearful or merely surviving, nor do we picture someone who is overwhelmed. The benefits of play occur when there is a sense of safety, when we can engage with another living thing with knowledge of being accepted while being true to ourselves. In this playfulness we are free to express joy and pleasure through words, touch, or eye contact.

The current research also suggests that developmental trauma may influence the level of playfulness we exhibit. This seems to be the case for other forms of trauma as well. Play has been used within a therapeutic context to treat PTSD in both children and adults because it connects to that healing ventral vagal system.

Coming from a Mennonite heritage that has a reputation of hard work and piety, play was not celebrated in my childhood. While I have some memories of play with friends and my sister, I don't have many memories of play with adults or of seeing adults at play. In general, it seems that adults tend to lose their ability to play. Is this because we no longer have the sense of safety needed for play? Are we mostly in the activated sympathetic state of survival or the dorsal vagal state of overwhelm? For the sake of healthier humans, let us play!

How Does Play Strengthen Our Nervous System?

Much like a muscle, our nervous system needs strength. It needs strength to do the hard things in life and it needs strength to persevere through long stretches of hard things. In a typical school setting, play is built into the day as recess or play activities because those are the moments that we integrate our new experiences and release the stress of learning new things. For adults, play can have the same benefits. Play can be the space our nervous system needs to take a breath and integrate the experiences of the day. Play can help us regulate the stresses of life.

The challenge is that for many of us, our playful childhood was a long time ago. In moments of survival, we can forget the value of play, or we may feel so overwhelmed with the weight of life that we feel that we can't imagine ourselves being free enough to play. We do not feel safe enough to play...yet.

Playfulness can start with an inner attitude of freedom and fun. As children develop play patterns, they start by playing by themselves, then playing by themselves but side by side with others, and eventually playing with others. The development of play allows the child to learn to read others for signs of safety and they learn the give-and-take of basic relationships. We call that co-regulation. This correlates to the development of the ventral vagal social engagement system mentioned earlier. In this final state of play, we are engaged with others and able to read their cues of safety. In healthy co-regulation, both parties are attuned to each others' nervous systems in a constantly changing flux of closeness and distance. Each party naturally helps the other manage emotions. We smile and laugh with the other and are sad and offer comfort when the other is suddenly injured. This is co-regulation.

Play releases happy hormones, giving us a sense of pleasure. An added benefit of these happy hormones is a decrease in pain and inflammation. Play literally takes the pain away! It is also interesting to note that play can make a significant difference in our genetic expression. The expression of genetics is called *epigenetics*. Play is powerful enough to make positive changes to your cells and help undo the genetic damage from the traumatic parts of life. That is incredible news for us and a powerful legacy for anyone passing on their genetics.

So, play is not frivolous escapism. Play is a necessity for life, vitality, and relationship with others.

Forms of Play

When was the last time you told a great joke? Reflecting on my largely unsafe childhood, I envied the funny kids. Playing with friends, occasionally someone would say, "tell us a joke!" I froze because of course I grew up in a house where ne'er a joke was told. I didn't really understand what was funny, how to make someone laugh, or how to build the storyline. I was the bummer in the group.

Humour is one component of playfulness that can be learned. Contrary to popular "find your mate" apps or teaching, humour is not a character trait that someone has or hasn't got. Rather, humour is an indicator of the ability of a person to engage in play. It turns out that at some level most of us still want connection with people who have a capacity for playfulness. We like people with a sense of humour. In other words, we like people who are in a ventral vagal state of safety. Surprise, surprise.

We can learn humour through practice. I am a proud auntie and those "kids" (some are adults at the time of this writing) have taught me a lot about play and fun, giving me an outlet to celebrate their playful, humorous, and creative parts while also celebrating and growing my own. One easy entry into humour is to tell knock-knock jokes to toddlers. They will laugh, you will gain confidence, and your nervous system will be strengthened as you break down the barriers to laughter and humour.

Using playful humour (not harsh, degrading humour as seems popular among some comedians), can also build depth to a relationship. Laughing together brings both parties into ventral vagal safety, allowing greater depth of intimacy in personal relationships as well as greater clarity of communication in personal, business, or any relationships. The reason communication becomes clearer is that both parties, now feeling safe, have their frontal lobe engaged. This allows them to understand what the other is saying, analyze it, and form a logical response, rather than react. Encouraging relational safety through humour can be a strong leadership tool.

Creativity is another element of play. Having a natural creative bent may be a character quality, but this too can be learned and explored. We may have a narrow definition of creativity that tells us that the visual arts are creative, but business leadership isn't. We may think poets are creative, but police officers aren't. We can grow a sense of creativity in any environment. This involves problem solving, literally making a product, or deciding to seize a moment with colour, song, or laughter.

During an extended family holiday, as the adults were watching the children ride around a small track in a train, their "crazy aunty" had an idea. Every time the train rolled past, I invited the adults to perform some crazy act or posture, such as the wave... nothing too strenuous! Of course, those kids loved it, as did the other families on the ride. Play is contagious and adds a ventral vagal sense of safety to more than just yourself. I didn't need a big creative project, I just needed to let my love for those kids flow freely through the act of play. A side benefit was a collective increase in ventral vagal safety in my family, at least for that moment, until a family adult, clearly uncomfortable with the notion of play (and ventral vagal safety), dismissively declared how silly I was. Of course, I took that as a compliment and badge of honour.

Is Gaming a Therapeutic Form of Play?

There are some challenges to online gaming as a form of play. Prolonged focus on the same distance, such as a screen, promotes a more dorsal vagal nervous system state. Although some games have a sense of danger requiring the gamer to dart their eyes back and forth across the screen, the distance the eyes move is not enough to communicate safety to the nervous system, and certainly not if the goal is to avoid some danger on the screen. The auditory stimulus associated with many games are rhythmical and toned in such a way to bring the gamer deeper into a state of automation and addiction that is more reflective of the dorsal vagal overwhelm state. This might be why a gamer feels a sense of escapism when playing, losing all sense of time and surroundings, because they have dissociated from reality, which is sometimes their point but is not healthful for their nervous system.

There may be some forms of gaming that can enhance nervous system health. If the game is played in cooperation or negotiation with others while not activating the fight-or-flight mechanism, it may help promote a sense of ventral vagal safety. However, this is not most online gaming.

It is also worth noting that care must be taken with any screen time. Screen time at any time of day encourages a fixed gaze, inviting us to a dorsal vagal state. When using a screen for any purpose we would do well to take frequent breaks to literally lift our eyes, gaze, and scan our eyes at a distance. The timing of screen time is also important in encouraging the innate circadian rhythms of sleep that help to guide our nervous systems. If possible, do not use screens for about six hours before you plan to sleep. At the very least, turn on the blue light filter when using them in the evening. The blue light mimics early morning sunshine and communicates to your nervous system that it is time to wake up. For more on this, please read the section on sleep.

Playfulness Exercises for Nervous System Safety and Resilience

➤ **First steps:** If the idea of playing is daunting to you, start with a little introduction to play. First, think back to a moment of play. This could be from your childhood. Try to remember a specific event, person, or place. Were you playing with a toy? What sights, sounds, or smells were around you? Can you feel the freedom and joy of that moment? Did you throw your head back in laughter? Did you jump for joy? What were the physical sensations in that moment of play?

With that memory in mind, look in a mirror and smile at yourself. Resist the temptation to be self-critical. Now make the biggest, goofiest smile you can. Give yourself the freedom to laugh at yourself and the silliness of this exercise. Try making goofy faces. Try to find at least five entirely different goofy facial expressions.

While still in front of the mirror, let yourself laugh out loud. Try it a little louder. Try it a little softer. Try it with a low belly laugh or a high-pitch giggle. Feel the sensations in your body as you try all the versions of laughter you can think of.

What do you notice about your nervous system as you did these exercises? Did any exercise invoke a genuine laugh? Did laughing feel strange? Did you notice the physical symptoms of joy that came from this exercise?

Next steps: Plan for play. In your daily, weekly, or monthly schedule, plan activities that increase your playfulness. Include play on your checklist if that feels empowering to you. Elevate the importance of playfulness in your schedule. This should not be left for any remnants of your life, because we rarely have those remnants. This doesn't have to be a significant time commitment like a pottery class, but it could be. Seeing it on your list reminds you to take a moment to laugh with a colleague, to tell a joke, to roll down the hill in a park, or to take a picture at the right angles to capture a creative view. Try different possibilities of play, like using your mind to play a game, or using your body to dance in a creative way.

When you schedule and experience fun, notice your body. Does your heart rate respond to fun? Is your internal temperature the same? Do you notice any other symptoms of tingling, warmth, or anything else? When you identify the physical sensation, then we can savour that sensation. This brings the experience to greater awareness, which allows us to remember these moments more easily. Our emotional memory system can often remember negative experiences more easily that pleasure and play. Savour the sensation of play so you can recall it later when it might give you strength or inspiration during a difficult time. The more detailed sensory experience of fun and play, the easier it will be for your nervous system to go back and remember safety, which is important for a resilient system.

Advanced steps: Integrating play into your life will be a regular reminder that your nervous system can feel the ease that allows play. This can be a simple thing such as listening to playful music as you do basic hygiene tasks. Or this can be dancing through your house rather than walking. If these suggestions seem like a bit of a reach, start small. Rather than dancing through your house, turn on some upbeat music you enjoy and dance with the upper half of your body. If you need to start smaller yet, try snapping your fingers to the beat or tapping your toes. Find some place in your body to feel the beat of the music and express it.

Try playfulness in a variety of ways. Play can be expressed through the mind, the body, the voice, or the hands. What are your easier ways of playing? What might be some new ways to explore play? If you are a singer, and are familiar with using your voice for play, what about the same mode of expression but completely different like beatboxing? If you are a crafter, being playful through your hands, maybe expand to using your hands to play a musical instrument? How does it feel to be playful using a completely new method?

Integrating play into daily life might also involve routines of playful activities. This might be a sport, a craft or hobby, ideally, in the company of others. Doing playful things with others allows us to practise safely co-regulating with others. This is important for increasing stability in our nervous system.

Spirituality

This book seeks to address how nervous system regulation is experienced in a broad range of life experiences. For that reason, I address the spiritual life as well. In this context, I don't assume any religious view, or even a view of the existence of a god. Theism and religion are not what I am describing as spirituality. You may, however, apply whatever spiritual viewpoints you have to the principles I will discuss.

Outside of a religious practice, spirituality can be thought of as that element that connects us to something bigger than ourselves. This might be a connection to a spiritual being or to a purpose or calling for our life. By its very nature, spirituality is deeply personal, often with a high level of conviction or passion. Because spirituality is deeply personal, different views can quickly create conflict and, thus, threat. What we do with those differences matter to our nervous system.

Let's review. When we see a threat, we will respond to the threat by shifting into sympathetic activation, the fight-or-flight response. We have left the safety of the ventral vagal moment and no longer feel safe. This can happen socially as people express their spirituality or deep convictions with others. Because these convictions are deeply held, there is great pressure for others to agree, resulting in those who don't agree becoming a threat. This threat keeps us in a sympathetic activation state, preventing us from accessing the health benefits of ventral vagal safety.

The current political climate capitalizes on those differing opinions and on our sympathetic fight-or-flight response by gaslighting us to see threats where there aren't any, or at the very least, where the threat is minimal. We are being gaslit to believe that others are evil and out to destroy us. This gaslighting creates passion and money for their cause. But it comes at a great cost to our nervous system. When we are gaslit to a cause, we enter the sympathetic state of danger, and we lose connection with our frontal lobes. This makes it even easier for the gaslighter to ask for more money and more sacrifice for their cause, and they gain followers, making the cause even more convincing.

The opposite of being gaslit is turning everything off, sticking our head in the sand, so to speak. This is not helpful either and it is more reflective of a dorsal vagal overwhelm state. We need to orient back to safety.

To orient to safety, we must assess the actual threat. If we think about the global trends, there may be aspects of societal shifts that may become a real threat. But there are a lot of those trends that have not yet become a real threat to us. We will need to hold the balance of seeing the safety that we have right now in this moment, with the potential threats we see around us. Our nervous system will be more rooted in ventral vagal safety if we approach these societal shifts as social justice, fighting for the good, rather than raging against an enemy.

A test of being gaslit is asking yourself if you still have empathy toward those involved in the issue being presented. Remember from the section on connection, empathy occurs when we are in safety. If our passion project or social justice cause brings us to an inability to have empathy, we have slipped into a sympathetic state.

A personal principle of mine is that I will not consider something at face value if the person telling it to me is raging in anger, communicating in a threatening manner, or is fixated on some mortal enemy. The reason for this is because I know that the amygdala in their brain is registering threat, which then turns off the thinking part of their brain. Information from raging people is more likely to be gaslighting your sympathetic nervous system to convince you of a threat that is not real, or not as imminent as the gaslighter suggests.

Spirituality can carry a great weight of importance. Taken in the context of purpose or vision, spirituality can be deeply empowering as this vision guides other aspects of life.

Living our vision or purpose has a level of excitement and empowering energy to it. This excitement and empowerment when we are living our vision and purpose is physiologically similar to the fight-or-flight response, except that there is no threat. We may feel an increase in heart rate or breathing rate when we are living our purpose. We feel an energetic desire to move forward in life, to accomplish goals. This can feel like the "flight" part of the fight-or-flight response, except that we are running toward a vision, rather than away from a threat. This empowered living can add strength to our nervous system, allowing us greater resilience to manage threats as they come.

Because living with passion and purpose physiologically feels like the fight-or-flight state, those who have frequently been in a sympathetic or dorsal vagal state may avoid passion and purpose. Our nervous systems have been programmed to avoid the sympathetic state, so we physiologically avoid passion and purpose as well. We rob ourselves of precious time living in our purpose because we have become so avoidant of the sensations of sympathetic activation. If that is your journey, from one traveller to another, there is still time to heal your nervous system and learn to savour the excitement of living your purpose and vision.

Spirituality Exercises for Nervous System Safety and Resilience

- **First steps:** Consider your spiritual practices. As you do the activities that are deeply "spiritual" to you, connect with yourself to determine what state you are in when doing them. Are you in ventral vagal safety as you sit in nature, contemplating the interconnectedness of the universe? Are you in sympathetic activation as you see all the people and groups that feel like a threat to your belief system? Are you in dorsal vagal state, unable to connect with your body as you go through the motions of a spiritual practice, theoretically present but not really?

➤ **Next steps:** As you become aware of your patterns of nervous system regulation in your spiritual practices, consider what changes you can make to allow your nervous system greater safety. Consider the threats you feel to your spirituality or purpose. Are they real and imminent to you? Is there a chance that you are being gaslit to see threats that don't really affect you or threats that have been blown out of proportion? How does your nervous system respond to people with different views? Do you have empathy toward people who don't share your views?

As you notice the response of your nervous system to different elements of your spiritual practice, are there elements that you'd like to eliminate, at least for now, or that you'd like to do more of, that will allow you to return to a ventral vagal state more easily? This should not be directed by obligation of religious practice or societal expectations. This should be directed by your nervous system as it shows you what it needs to deepen a sense of ventral vagal safety.

➤ **Advanced steps:** If you have not already done it, consider your vision and purpose in life. If the mere suggestion of determining a purpose for your life gives you anxiety, tune in to your nervous system to feel the anxiety. Is the anxiety related to something specific? Is there a way that you can consider a vision or purpose that doesn't give you anxiety? Rather than potential baggage from the past, consider vision and purpose as the direction and fuel for nervous system safety with action.

If a sense of vision or purpose doesn't immediately come to you as you contemplate it, you can go through your day, week, and month as a compassionate observer of your nervous system. Watch for those signs of passion such as an increased heart rate, a spontaneous smile, or a sudden burst of productive energy. When you notice these things, consider the common threads and the tasks you are doing. Your purpose or vision might be related to those moments.

Find a way to articulate this vision and passion. Decide what that next step is to live more fully in that purpose. This should not be a to-do list that will contaminate your purpose with ways to self-condemn. This should be something that will allow you to better see and experience your purpose. It is about living the purpose, rather than doing a purpose. It is about living your very best life.

Conclusion

THE BEAUTY AND LEARNING OF life are more about the journey than they are about the destination. The journey to finding more safety and resilience in our nervous systems can be the same way. There will be hills to climb, beautiful vistas, moments of defeat and of celebration. Creating more safety and resilience is the journey, not the destination.

I am an imperfect traveller on this journey. I have moments that last longer than they should when I am in an appropriate state. I have seasons when I have to fight harder to come back to a state of safety. But the more I understand about the effect of the nervous system on my life, the more I can come back to safety. Before I understood the effect of my nervous system, I would stay in a dorsal vagal state much longer, telling myself how much of a failure I was. Occasionally, those self-assessments had a grain of truth to them, but most often, my nervous system was letting me see only one side of the story. In those moments, I could use these exercises to pull myself out of that "funk" so I could see reality for what it was and make better decisions next time.

Experiencing safety in your nervous system is a life-altering experience. It can be like starting a beautiful friendship. At first, it might feel awkward and strange. But, over time, there is deep comfort and understanding. Experiencing safety in your nervous system can be like that. Having a greater ability to get back to ventral vagal safety after something throws us into a threat response is empowering. Knowing when we are ramping up into a threat response is enlightening and gives us the kind invitation to heal deeper.

Now that you have travelled a bit of this journey, you may notice expansive opportunities in other parts of your life. Hard things may not feel as heavy. Difficult people may not affect you as deeply or as long. You may become healthier as you literally move more, and you might crave more or deeper social connections. We are all on this journey together. There is no ideal final destination and the notion of having a fully resilient nervous system is a myth. Our resilience ebbs and flows as life happens. We seek not to attain a fictional state of health, but to continue in greater awareness and greater resilience whether we are in the pit of despair or thriving.

Wherever you are in your journey toward a more resilient nervous system, I hope you enjoy the journey and celebrate the big and small shifts in your life. Cheers to a more resilient nervous system!

ADDITIONAL RESOURCES

About Your Nervous System

Dana, D. (2018). *The Polyvagal Theory in Therapy: Engaging the Rhythm of Regulation (Norton series on interpersonal neurobiology)*. WW Norton & Company.

Levine, P. A. (1997). *Waking the Tiger: Healing Trauma: The innate capacity to transform overwhelming experiences*. North Atlantic Books.

Porges, S. W. (2011). *The Polyvagal Theory: Neurophysiological Foundations of Emotions, Attachment, Communication, and Self-regulation (Norton series on interpersonal neurobiology)*. WW Norton & Company.

About Your Body: Safety and Resilience

Emerson, D. (2015). *Trauma-Sensitive Yoga in Therapy: Bringing the Body into Treatment*. WW Norton & Company.

Schwartz, A. (2020). *The Complex PTSD Workbook: A Mind-body Approach to Regaining Emotional Control and Becoming Whole*. Sheldon Press.

Siegel, D. J. (2009). "Mindful Awareness, Mindsight, and Neural Integration." *The Humanistic Psychologist, 37*(2), 137–158.

Treleaven, D. A. (2018). *Trauma-sensitive Mindfulness: Practices for Safe and Transformative Healing*. WW Norton & Company.

About Your Gut: Safety and Resilience

Korn, L. (2016). *Nutrition Essentials for Mental Health: A Complete Guide to the Food-mood Connection.* WW Norton & Company.

Mayer, E. A., & Burns, T. (2016). *The Mind-gut Connection: How the Hidden Conversation Within Our Bodies Impacts Our Mood, Our Choices, and Our Overall Health.* New York: Harper Wave.

Perlmutter, D. (2018). *Grain Brain: The Surprising Truth about Wheat, Carbs, and Sugar—Your Brain's Silent Killers.* Hachette UK.

Scott, T. (2011). *The Antianxiety Food Solution: How the Foods You Eat Can Help You Calm Your Anxious Mind, Improve Your Mood, and End Cravings.* New Harbinger Publications.

Dirty Dozen Foods: https://www.smallfarmcanada.ca/news/2022-dirty-dozen-and-clean-15-released/

About Your Life: Safety and Resilience

Kain, K. L., & Terrell, S. J. (2018). *Nurturing Resilience: Helping Clients Move Forward from Developmental Trauma—An Integrative Somatic Approach.* North Atlantic Books.

Rosenberg, S. (2017). *Accessing the Healing Power of the Vagus Nerve: Self-help Exercises for Anxiety, Depression, Trauma, and Autism.* North Atlantic Books.

Siegel, D. J. (2010). *Mindsight: The New Science of Personal Transformation.* Bantam.

Stanley, E. A. (2019). *Widen the Window: Training Your Brain and Body to Thrive During Stress and Recover from Trauma.* Penguin.

GLOSSARY OF TERMS

Activation – Activation occurs when your nervous system moves from the restful ventral vagal state to the sympathetic state of movement or *fight-or-flight*. This can happen because of perceived danger (triggered) or without danger, as a sense of excitement.

Anchors – Anchors are the objects, visualizations, or sensations that can remind us that we have a body, and that we are in present time. Anchors help bring us back to ventral vagal safety.

Autonomic Nervous System – The autonomic nervous system includes the parts of the brain that regulate all the functions that we don't actively think about. This includes breathing, digestion, etc. It is further divided into the sympathetic nervous system that activates the fight-or-flight responses, and the parasympathetic nervous system that calms the sympathetic nervous system.

Biopsychosocial Model – This model illustrates the influences of the body, the brain (thoughts and emotions), and the relational environment we are in. These factors influence each other and cannot be viewed in isolation for effective healing.

Boundaries – Boundaries, in this context, refer to knowledge of the edges of ourselves, especially in relation to others. Expression of those boundaries may include telling people what you need or don't need.

Circadian Rhythm – Circadian rhythm is the sleep-wake schedule naturally embedded into our bodies. This includes the nervous system and the hormonal system.

Co-regulation – Co-regulation happens because of empathy, where two people (or creatures) are connecting with each other assessing danger by reading the other person's cues. This happens simultaneously with both people.

Dissociation – In this context, I am *not* talking about clinical dissociation. In this context, I am talking about the phenomenon that happens when we lose awareness of ourselves. This often happens in a dorsal vagal overwhelm state.

Dorsal Vagal – The dorsal vagal state is directed by the dorsal (back) fibres of the vagus nerve that originates from the nucleus ambiguus, in the medulla of the brainstem. It is part of the parasympathetic nervous system. The dorsal vagal state is one of overwhelm and is triggered by danger or stress that is too large to be processed as it is happening, or danger or stress that occurs over too long a period of time. It is an energetic recovery state. This is sometimes referred to as the freeze response.

Dysregulation – Dysregulation happens when we are either stuck in an inappropriate nervous system state or we inappropriately jump into another nervous system state. For example, we reach exhaustion and can't recover to pull out of the dorsal vagal state. Or, we jump into a sympathetic danger state when no danger exists.

Electromagnetic Field – Because we have electronically charged particles flowing through our bodies, we have an electromagnetic field. This can be felt when someone you can't see comes up behind you and you can sense them "in your space." This is because your electromagnetic field interacted with theirs.

Fight-or-Flight – The fight-or-flight response occurs when the nervous system perceives danger and activates the sympathetic nervous system. The danger does not need to be real or present in this moment for the response to occur. This can be a physical threat or emotional threat.

Guardrails – Guardrails refer to the feedback and exercises you can use to keep yourself within your window of tolerance.

Gut Biome/Microbiome – The microbiome or gut biome is the community of naturally occurring living things within your gut, or your intestines. The function of the gut biome is to create balance, allowing absorption of the nutrients you need while also communicating to your brain about your health.

Gut-brain Axis – This axis refers to the information pathway between your gut and your brain. The gut has many receptors that give feedback to the brain.

Heart Rate Variability – Heart rate variability (HRV) is the phenomena of an increase in heart rate during an in breath, and a slowing down of heart rate during an out breath. The increase with inhalation is related to a slight increase in sympathetic activation and the decrease with exhalation is related to an increase in parasympathetic activation.

Interoception – Interoception is the process of becoming aware of what is happening inside yourself. This can include awareness of breath and heart rate, or awareness of emotion or physical tension.

Mindfulness – Mindfulness is a practice of increasing awareness. This can be an increased awareness of your own self or your surroundings and can be on multiple levels, such as the five physical senses or in an intuitive sense.

Nervous System State – Nervous system states are either sympathetic or parasympathetic. We divide parasympathetic into two other states: ventral vagal and dorsal vagal. When we ask what nervous system state we are in, it is not an all or nothing, but it is asking which state is dominant in this moment.

Neuroplasticity – Neuroplasticity refers to the brain's ability to change and adapt to new stimuli and new demands.

Overwhelm – An overwhelm state is another way to say dorsal vagal state.

Proprioception – Proprioception is the process that your body knows where you are in your environment. Are you standing, sitting, lying down? Are you moving or stationary? Are you walking on uneven ground?

Resilience – Resilience is the force needed to overcome adversity, to adapt to a changing environment, and to grow.

Spirituality – In this context we are not referring to religion, but the aspect of life that connects to a meaning and purpose.

Sympathetic Nervous System – The sympathetic nervous system is the gas pedal. This is the nervous system that becomes activated in danger or excitement.

Under-aroused – Being under-aroused is in reference to your window of tolerance where there is not enough stimulus to keep you engaged in your life. This can result in depression.

Vagus Nerve – The vagus nerve is the tenth cranial nerve. It starts in two distinct nuclei in the brain, travels down the neck, chest and belly, sending branches to most organs along the way. The vagus nerve acts as the brake to the sympathetic nervous system to help calm us down.

Ventral Vagal – Ventral vagál is the state of calm, peace, and safety that allows for good digestion and connection with others.

Window of Tolerance – The window of tolerance is the breadth of stimulation we can tolerate before we are either under-aroused or overstimulated. The window of tolerance is our window of optimal function. A small window of tolerance does not allow much variation in stimulation before compromising our ability to function.

Printed in Canada